SUMMIT LEADERSHIP

TAKING YOUR TEAM TO THE TOP

A RICH DAD ADVISOR BOOK

SUMMIT LEADERSHIP

TAKING YOUR TEAM TO THE TOP

BLAIR SINGER

FOREWORD BY ROBERT KIYOSAKI

This publication is designed to provide competent and reliable information regarding the subject matter covered. However, it is sold with the understanding that the author and publisher are not engaged in rendering legal, financial, or other professional advice. Laws and practices often vary from state to state and country to country and if legal or other expert assistance is required, the services of a professional should be sought. The author and publisher specifically disclaim any liability that is incurred from the use or application of the contents of this book.

Published by RDA Press, LLC
Rich Dad Advisors, B-I Triangle, CASHFLOW Quadrant and other Rich Dad marks are registered trademarks of CASHFLOW Technologies, Inc.

RDA Press LLC
15170 N. Hayden Road
Scottsdale, AZ 85260
480-998-5400
Visit our Web sites: RDA-Press.com and BlairSinger.com

Printed in Canada
First Edition: April 2022

ISBN: 978-1-937832-69-8

052022

Summit Leadership

Taking Your Team to the Top

Lessons from 5895 meters

Foreword
by Robert Kiyosaki

What Is Leadership?

Leadership is power. And a simple definition of power is "the ability to do."

That definition describes my long-time friend Blair Singer. Blair has the unreal ability and the power to inspire others "to do" the impossible, to go beyond their personal limitations, thoughts, and beliefs... to climb to the top of Kilimanjaro.

But life is *not* about making it to the top of Kilimanjaro. Kilimanjaro is outside of us. Life is about summitting and conquering the peaks of Kilimanjaro *inside of us* — those daunting and seemingly insurmountable challenges and obstacles that life throws at us on a daily basis. That is Blair's amazing ability and where his genius shines.

When Blair leads everyday people, people like you and me, to the top of Kilimanjaro, he is inspiring each of us — ordinary people — to first be leaders of ourselves, leaders in our personal lives... *before* we can lead others.

In their book *The Fourth Turning* (1998), a book of prophecy, authors William Straus and Neil Howe warn of the Fourth Turning, a period in which we find ourselves today, in 2022. Strauss and Howe emphasize that the Fourth Turning will be a period marked by weak "leaders." Observing the news of the past few years, the United States of America in turning into the Divided States of America... with the burning of cities, looting sprees, a humiliating retreat from Afghanistan, open-border invasions, mass migrations, workers refusing to be vaccinated in the faces of government mandates... and on and on. Do we need more proof that the world is in a Fourth Turning, and that it is a leaderless world?

Blair Singer's book *Summit Leadership* is the complement to *The Fourth Turning*. In a world of weak leaders, it is more important than ever that we draw all we can from Blair's lifetime of study, real life experience, and his wisdom on the subject of leadership. Increasing your personal leadership skills may be your most important investment during this time in history.

Always remember, leadership is power. And your most important power is your ability to lead yourself... before you lead others.

Robert Kiyosaki

Contents

Introduction

Life is full of lessons. The universe throws challenges, obstacles, and rewards your way constantly as if there were some pre-determined life curricula of study you are supposed to take and master. Only you have no syllabus to follow, no agenda, no list of assignments to be completed. You may find yourself flying by the seat of your pants, hoping for an A but winding up with a C, D, or an F more often than not.

Then it's back to life's classroom. I have often wondered why we get the set of lessons that we get. It's like we become magnets for a certain set of lessons, almost like a kind of fatal attraction. But why?

What I do know is if you don't learn the lesson being presented to you, you will be forced to deal with it again and again, at ever-increasing intensity, until you finally get it. Unfortunately, by the time you start to master some of life's lessons, your time is already counting down.

Your lessons will come from every area of your life: your health, your family, your kids, your friends, your business, your teams. As you are a student of life, so is everyone else. Sometimes the lessons will be the same, but the timing will be different. Sometimes the lessons themselves will be different. Think of it as being in a one-room schoolhouse where everyone is learning at their own level and pace. And if the whole of your experiences is like a school, the good news is that you have teachers to fall back on, and the better news is that YOU are also a teacher to others who have yet to learn the lessons you've mastered.

I firmly believe our purpose, as leaders, is to do just that. It's to master the lessons and then pass that knowledge on to others so that they might accelerate their own learning journeys. That as each generation of business leaders, community leaders, thought leaders, spiritual leaders, health, wealth, and happiness leaders learn through trial and error, we empower those on our teams and within our circles of influence to reach even higher levels of achievement, growth, and happiness.

A remarkable person I met years ago, whom I consider a great teacher, is a man named Po Chung. He is the co-founder of DHL International. One day, in his Hong Kong office, we discussed the importance of 'Leaders being Teachers.' I feel he hit the nail on the head when he said, "It is a business leader's *societal responsibility* to teach whatever they have learned in their careers to others." This is what moves our civilization and species ahead.

I have committed this part of my career and life to training the best teachers and leaders in the world to expedite the transfer of knowledge and fundamentally change the way we learn and grow, particularly in the marketplace.

In 2012, I had a unique opportunity to travel to Africa with my then 16-year-old son, Ben, and climb Mt. Kilimanjaro. I've been back eight times since. I didn't go there expecting to learn leadership lessons, but that's exactly what happened. Each trip up the mountain taught me something unique and transformative about true leadership. This doesn't happen for everyone. It happened for me, and it happens for those I take up the mountain each year because I had excellent teachers in our mountain guides Kevin Cherilla and Kristen Sandquist of K2 Adventure Travel. Those first few years of climbing with them, I'm not even sure they knew how valuable their lessons were.

The thirteen-day trip to Africa and the top of Mt. Kilimanjaro, is one of the most exquisite, intense, and profound microcosms of a person's life. The trek up the mountain forces you out of complacency, out of the hypnotic rhythm of everyday life, and makes you acutely aware of everything around you. The weather, your physicality, even your mental state can change in a heartbeat. You must make decisions and adapt quickly or fail. The lessons of leadership come fast and furious. They are embedded in every step, every breath, and every connection with your fellow hikers, with nature, and your inner being. So much so that the only guarantee I give to those who trek there with my team is that the person who comes off that mountain will be the biggest and best version of themselves.

As leaders, we all have mountains to climb in our business and our personal lives. And while you may not be able to ascend to a physical summit and back, you can still reap the benefits of the lessons from Kilimanjaro. You can kick it up a notch. You can become acutely aware. You can come full circle from being a learner to being a teacher and bettering your team. That's why I decided to write this book—to share the leadership lessons I've learned on the mountain with all of you who are ready to tackle your summit, whatever that may be.

At present, we are locked in a global crisis that includes a pandemic, economic collapse, and the possible restructuring of how humanity will live its life. These are our Kilimanjaros. This period will be remembered, good and bad, for many generations to come. The biggest lesson the future will look back upon is what leadership emerged, or did not emerge, during these times.

I feel blessed to be living at this amazing juncture in the history of humankind. The future will determine how well we led. How well we raised our families. How well we built and supported our teams and communities. How courageously we continued to love, connect, teach, and learn the lessons that have been provided to us.

One of my mentors said it well. "Crisis is change trying to come forth." A crisis appears because the invitations to make changes are ignored or pushed down the road for convenience, comfort, or ignorance. We are in a crisis, and now change has demanded our attention. It is my hope and intention that the lessons of leadership at 19,341 feet (5900 meters) on Kilimanjaro inspire you to make the right calls, do the right things, and lead your families, teams, and communities to new heights of success and fulfillment...not just for you, but for all of us.

I found my answer to why you seem to have a 'fatal attraction' to a certain set of lessons...it's because you are a leader. That's it. And your job is to use those lessons to serve the greatest number of people you can. It's because, in your DNA, you are supposed to lead. You've known it for a long time. You may have been reluctant or afraid to admit it. But you would not be reading this if something didn't pull you toward it.

Whether it's Kilimanjaro, Covid-19, economic turmoil, or raising your family, here are the lessons that will be the mountain guide for reaching your and your team's summit.

Lead with knowledge, courage, and inspiration!

Blair

Chapter One

Leadership at 18,652 Feet

*"Only those who will risk going too far can possibly find out
how far one can go."*

—*T.S. Eliot*

July 11, 2019
Stella Point, Kilimanjaro
18,652 Feet Above Sea Level
Just Below the Summit

The mountain climbing guide's eyes widen and convey a message I don't want to hear. Through the howling wind, her words ring crystal clear.

"You gotta go down the mountain, NOW!" Kristen commands. "Go now!"

Her pulse oximeter shows my blood oxygen level had begun to drop precipitously. Dangerous!! When that happens, climbers are rapidly sent back down the mountain to a lower elevation where their lungs can draw more oxygen. If I don't get down quickly, my lungs and brain could fill with fluid. Edema, unconsciousness... even death could occur.

Yet, I don't even feel too bad right now. I feel like I can make it to the summit, which is less than 700 feet up. But I also know the rules. Kristen is the guide—the leader. Her word is LAW! If I disobey her, I may jeopardize not only my life but my teammates' lives as well.

Shit! I've successfully climbed this mountain eight times before. Why is this happening now? And what am I going to do with this banner?

The banner I'm holding is supposed to be unfurled at the summit—it's a tradition for climbs I organize. Suddenly, my brain goes quiet; everything goes into slow motion. I know what I have to do and every second counts. I quickly survey our thirty climbers and toss the banner to Pao—a bright, young Malaysian woman who teaches meditation.

"I've gotta go," I say to her, not having time to explain.

My head now feels like a balloon, and my vision is distorted. Kristen was right. I need to go down. Fast!

I follow Ali, one of our amazing Tanzanian porters, who breaks into a full run down the mountain. He's carrying my backpack and, presumably, would carry me should I collapse. Ali, with his deeply scarred face and a beaming smile, is a pleasure to be around, even though he speaks very little English. He comes from a meager background and spends his entire year scraping together what money he can for the high season of climbing when he can serve others. The amount of work he does and the strength he has is uncommon for a man of his small size. Whenever there is a time to dance and sing, his baritone voice booms with volume and joy. Right now, he has reverted to his instinctive behavior to serve, save lives, and do whatever it takes at the moment. In this moment, that's getting me down this mountain.

The six to eighteen inches of soft volcanic scree and ash beneath our feet churn up huge clouds of dust as we run. Fortunately, a brisk wind from the east keeps the dust out of our faces. I should explain that the trail hikers use to come down the mountain is not the same trail they use to go up. The upward climb is a rocky trail that would be impossible to run without hurting yourself. I'm grateful for the cushioned descent as I run for my life.

Not a cloud in the sky. The sun is shining. I'm sweating like a pig. My lungs are heaving for more air. My quads are on fire. Ali and I will run for nearly an hour to reach our summit base camp Kosovo at 15,748 feet. *Will I make it?*

My thoughts turn to my wife and boys. It's true what people say. When you face death, you don't think about work or your accomplishments. You think about the ones you love.

For me, this included my son, Ben, from whom I learned priceless lessons about leadership and fatherhood seven years earlier when he and I took our first trek up Africa's highest mountain.

◆ ◆ ◆ ◆ ◆

The year was 2012.

Ben was 16—a junior in high school in Phoenix, Arizona. He was a good student, good athlete, and his teachers loved him. He was, and is, an all-around great kid. But like many boys his age, Ben and some buddies decided to pull a prank at school that turned out not to be as funny as they had anticipated. It caused quite a bit of turmoil and chaos. Ben had never been in trouble before, and the consequences of his actions left him devastated.

I remember telling him at the time, "Everyone makes mistakes. That's how you learn. That is life. This incident can be the worst thing that ever happens to you or the best. Your choice!"

One of the resolutions of the incident was an agreement for Ben to seek and perform community service. I knew I needed to find a way to lift this kid up. He needed to be in new surroundings; he needed a new mission; he needed to feel he could do something good with his life. So, when a stranger I met on a flight back from New York told me about K2 Adventure Travel in Scottsdale, Arizona, and the service opportunities they had around the globe, I had to call.

K2 founders and co-owners Kevin Cherilla and Kristen Sandquist are experienced climbers who also operate a nonprofit foundation to raise money for kids and families with disabilities in Arizona, Nepal, Peru, and Tanzania. In the last five years, they have raised over 2.5 million dollars for medical equipment, resources, and supplies in Tanzania alone. They gained international notoriety when they led an expedition of eight blind climbers to the summit of Kilimanjaro.

Ironically, it was that challenge that brought Kevin and Kristen together to form K2. Kevin had been asked to take these eight individuals up the mountain but he knew he needed an assistant guide. He was introduced to Kristen through a mutual friend. Her desire for serving others piqued her interest in the challenge and she said, "Sure, I'll go. What's that mean? Do we have to sleep in tents?" Little did she know. Kristen had never slept in a tent, had never even slept in a sleeping bag before. Regardless, they both took eight blind people all the way to the top of Kilimanjaro and set a world record for doing so. That began their business partnership, and hence the name K2, Kevin and Kristen. Their spouses and children are fully supportive of the work they do.

But they don't just raise money. I found K2 has an amazing orphanage for kids with disabilities in Tanzania, where we could volunteer to work. Along with the ability to be of service to these kids, they include climbing to the summit of Kilimanjaro. For Kevin and Kristen, the mountain represents the even bigger mountains these kids have to climb either to stay alive or to have a life; mountains of disease, abandonment, blindness, poverty, and lack of education. The climb would be an ordeal, perhaps the hardest thing we would do in our lifetimes. Ben and I liked the idea.

In July 2012, we headed to Tanzania, where we joined a dozen climbers from the U.S. who also were making the seven-day trek to the summit with K2. But first, we all volunteered at the orphanage for two days, helping in the garden, cleaning, and making repairs. It was fun and life-changing. It reminded us how great it is to help others and how those with so little can be so happy and grateful. We felt deep gratitude for being able to somehow play a role in the lives of these amazing children.

The first day climbing the mountain was strenuous and long but beautiful, as we progressed through the rain forest to nearly 10,000 feet. But in the middle of that night on the mountain, Ben got sick. REAL SICK. He started vomiting uncontrollably. It may have been something he ate, some nasty malaria medicine, or dehydration. We didn't know.

After a very rough night, we attempted to keep going the next morning. But to no avail. He was still vomiting, his eyes were turning yellow, and he was very weak. We had gotten just above the cloud line when it became clear he had to go back down.

One of our porters could have taken him down to a clinic, and I could have continued the climb. My normal inclination would have been to keep going to achieve my goal. In that rarified air, looking at my son, looking at the summit, and looking into my heart, I was torn. Yet, I remembered a rule that had been part of my personal code of honor for many years that I nearly forgot: "Never abandon a teammate in need." I would take him down. I would not abandon Ben now.

When we reached the foot of the mountain, medical staff at a clinic rehydrated Ben with an intravenous solution. Eighteen hours later, he was feeling better.

I was relieved.

The incident taught me a priceless lesson about being a real father. It taught me the trajectory of our lives are driven by things bigger and more powerful than mountains. One of those things is love. Mountains last for centuries, but the relationship with my son is fleeting in the cosmos. Without that rule (the importance of which we will discuss later), I might have made a catastrophically bad decision at 10,000 feet.

We returned home and I figured our mountain climbing days were over.

But several months later, Ben approached me and said, "Dad, I want to go back to Kilimanjaro."

"Why?" I asked.

"Because not a day goes by when I don't think about that mountain kicking my ass." His courage filled me with pride.

We returned the following summer. That first trek up the mountain had taught us another lesson: We hadn't had enough time to train and we hadn't been prepared. This time we were. At 11:30 am Tanzania time on July 3, 2013, Ben and I successfully hit the summit. We hugged, we laughed, we cried, we made it!

I reached into my backpack to give Ben a gift I had been carrying the whole way up the mountain. It was a key chain with an inscribed pendant. On one side, it said,

"Kilimanjaro 2012-2013"

On the other side,

"We start together and we finish together." – Dad

When I gave it to him I told him that I would always have his back.

On that day, my son and I reconnected in a way that I never dreamed possible.

I had no idea a mountain could teach me to be a better father. That's the thing about the mountain; you can never predict what kind of lessons it will teach you. Every time I go, I learn something new about myself and others.

The journey also reinforced the idea, which I emphasize in my programs, that big goals are difficult to obtain without a team. This applies not just to one's personal life but business as well. Yet, to accomplish those goals and to assemble and move a team forward requires great leadership. How to be a great leader is not taught in school. Good role models are difficult to find. But those who become dedicated students of leadership will learn it and succeed. And if we are associated with them, we win too. This book will show you how.

On the way down the mountain with Ben that day, I was bubbling like a kid in a toy store. The mountain had taught me so much. Watching our guides, Kevin and Kristen, take a relatively inexperienced group from different walks of life safely up and down this mountain, I realized this journey offered amazing lessons not commonly taught in most leadership programs.

How in the world did they get all of us "flat-landers" and newbies safely up and down one of the largest mountains in the world? How could I accomplish that kind of magic in my own business teams?

"You guys are a different kind of teacher," I told Kevin and Kristen. "I would love to come back and bring with me some of my friends, colleagues, and participants of some of my seminars."

They loved the idea. We call it the "Mountain Leadership Experience."

For the next seven years, I journeyed back to Kilimanjaro, bringing with me each time dozens of businesspeople and professionals recruited from seminars I have given around the world.

As a team, each of us agrees to a set of rules designed to protect ourselves and the team during the climb. We also pledge to obey Kevin and Kristen, our guides. Rules are crucial for achieving goals.

In July 2019, on my ninth trip to the mountain, my commitment to these and other leadership principles was tested.

Our group reached Kosovo base camp, where we camped for the night. We would trek to the summit the following day.

♦ ♦ ♦ ♦ ♦

Midnight, July 10, 2019
Kosovo Base Camp
The evening before the summit trek and Stella Point

The nylon fabric in my tent is flapping violently from winds gusting to fifty miles per hour. The sound is deafening. I can't sleep. But even if the air were calm, I'd probably be awake.

I usually have trouble sleeping on the eve before embarking on the final 2,500-vertical foot ascent to Kilimanjaro's summit, partly because I am filled with wonder and excitement.

Fear too.

The air's thin up here—so thin the lack of oxygen can hurt you. Early signs of altitude sickness include disorientation, lethargy, headache, and nausea. Without heeding the warnings, you can lose consciousness and slip into a coma. Every year, a small handful of people die climbing Kilimanjaro. That's not a lot when you consider 40,000 climbers attempt the journey every year.

But I've seen what happens to climbers with severe altitude sickness. Guides and porters often have to carry or help them down the mountain. They look bad—real bad, like 'road-kill,' even zombie-like.

This evening I feel nauseated and have a slight headache. Probably nothing, but I err on the side of caution and take an additional altitude pill—Diamox—which helps my body expel carbon dioxide and increase oxygen in my blood.

I also take an anti-nausea pill. I've never taken it before, but it seems to work. I drift off, feeling the power and the majesty of the mountain and the elements all around me. But my slumber doesn't last long. I wake again at 2:30 am.

In a half-hour, mountain guides will rouse the other two-dozen climbers in our group. I might as well dress now.

Should I wear my snow pants with suspenders?

They are comfortable, but when you need to crap on the trail, you to have to remove most of your upper-body clothing. This morning the wind-chill temperature is probably 10 degrees Fahrenheit.

Maybe I can do my business before leaving base camp.

I dress—a task that takes about twenty minutes at this altitude. Heavy wool socks, thick boots, gaiters, insulated underwear, a silk shirt, snow pants (with suspenders), a lightweight "poofy" down jacket with a hood, an insulating beanie with a headlamp, and a waterproof hooded jacket.

"Good morning," one of the porters says outside my tent promptly at 3 am. "Time to rise."

"I'm up," I reply.

Several minutes later, I crawl out of my protective cocoon. The sky is clear. It takes my breath away. Not because of the cold, but because of the millions of stars over me. This mountain connects you to the universe in a way no other vantage point can. It's more than amazing—it's spiritual. That's partly why I keep coming back.

The camp is dark, except for narrow beams of light coming from the headlamps of a dozen or so climbers preparing for the day's journey.

I feel better now. The medicine must be working.

This is going to be the best climb of all. I am ready to roll. I make my way to the meal tent for some hot porridge.

"Hey, boss," says Singer, one of our porters who has the same surname as me but pronounces it "Singa."

The altitude has little effect on him and the other porters, who have acclimated to the thin air, which has half the oxygen available at sea level. They carry most of our gear, which includes tents and supplies and five-gallon buckets of water.

After breakfast, I work on a BM but with no success. *That's strange.* I hope my decision to wear the suspenders doesn't come back to haunt me. Our group leaves promptly at 5 am.

Kristen takes the lead. Kevin takes the sweep. I'm in the group behind Kristen. To acclimatize to the altitude, we move very slowly.

Rest step...pressure breathe, rest step...pressure breathe...

The process is repeated every couple of seconds in a slow, deliberate rhythm. Pressure breathing is the intense exhaling action that expels carbon dioxide from our bodies, which increases oxygen in the blood. It's uncomfortable for beginners. But everyone catches on.

We proceed at a rate of less than 1 mile per hour—about a fourth or third as fast as most people walk. We'll take a break every 50-60 minutes on the way up. It's hard work. Really hard! My Little Voice is going crazy. "Maybe I can't make it. I can't seem to move my legs..."

After the fourth break, I am beginning to feel sick again. Lightheaded. My quads feel stiff, heavy, depleted.

But Stella Point, the first summit, is only 20 minutes away. I know I can make it.

Stella Point—10:00 am

We reach Stella Point, which is 689 feet in elevation below the high summit. The porters serve us hot tea that they carried up for us.

I still feel lightheaded, but better. I know I can make it.

Kristen is going around the group and testing each climber's oxygen levels. She reaches me, and after taking my reading, she says: "You feeling OK?"

"Not too bad," I reply.

"Why don't you take another 250 milligrams of Diamox, and I'll check you in a few minutes?"

I comply because she is the leader. She is one of our mountain guides and when she looks at you with her deep, dark brown, piercing eyes you know she means business. Kristen is trained as a first mountain responder. When other hikers get into trouble, even if they are not a part of her group, she and her business partner Kevin are the first to get the call. When it comes to safety and health, she is no joke; her voice is law.

To see her on the street in Scottsdale, AZ you'd never guess she helps others to climb some of the highest mountains in the world for a living. Kristen is attractive, with a bright smile, an athletic build, and her blonde hair typically pulled back in a ponytail. For over 25 years she has built and run her own nonprofits serving special needs children and families worldwide. It is no surprise she has carried on that legacy with K2.

She returns after a few minutes and takes another reading. Her eyeballs turn the size of saucers. She issues the order for me to descend and....

Ali and I begin our race down the mountain.

We reach Camp Kosovo about an hour later. I'm exhausted. I get something to drink and sit.

I feel bad for being separated from the group. Supporting the team is important to me. But I also do not question Kristen's decision. She knows what she is doing.

I go to my tent. I still feel loopy. My head feels big. I check my own oxygen level—Still dropping!!!

Oh my God! I've got to get out of here, or I'm going to die.

I strip off my outer clothes and throw them into my mountain bag. Ali throws all the gear on his back, and we take off at high speed to get farther down the mountain.

My head feels like it's the size of a truck.

Nearly two hours later, we reach Millenium Camp at 12,000 feet. I check my oxygen again—rising now.

Thank goodness.

I guzzle some tea and a liter of water and I lie down in my tent. I sleep for three hours. When I wake, I'm several points higher. I feel much better.

When the rest of the team arrives after making the summit, I'm nearly back to normal. But it takes me several weeks to fully recover.

Needless to say, I am disappointed in not reaching the summit. But, as I've taught others before, **Leadership is not about always reaching the summit.**

It's about the people or team you are with. It's about helping each other—it's the life-changing lessons you learn along the way, the sights, the people, the opportunities, insights, and connections that live with you forever. It's about the journey. Despite the setback, this journey was one of the best. Learning when to stand down and trust those leading me was a huge lesson in my own leadership development.

When I returned home, I went to my doctor, who ran tests and couldn't find anything physically wrong with me. Did my oxygen level drop because of the nausea medication I took? Or was I just exhausted? Or constipated?

Or was it simply old age? After all, I'm in my sixties now (but don't tell anyone). I stay in shape, but are my climbing days over?

These questions and others swirled in my head as I tried to figure out what happened. The only thing I was sure of was that Kristen had made the right call, and the rules she and Kevin had created were based on sound leadership. When I asked Kristen why I had failed, she was crystal clear. "You broke the rules. You took medication that you have never taken before and you did not consult me before doing so!" I'll be talking a lot more about the importance of rules in a later chapter.

Rules protect us from ourselves. Many of us are afraid to fail in our personal and business lives, so we push ourselves to great extremes, sometimes jeopardizing not only our own safety but those around us. Entrepreneurs are often guilty of this. When their business begins to fail, they often don't know when to throw in the towel. They keep pouring money, time, and energy into a failing venture, only to crash and burn and feel even worse when they look around at the collateral damage to their teams, families, and themselves.

Remember, getting to the top is only halfway there and is optional. Coming down safely to family, friends, and community is mandatory.

A good leader recognizes that failure is a necessary element to achieving ultimate success. There are times when he or she must let things go and move on. Cut your losses. Learn from your mistakes, and either make significant changes or start anew.

Phil Knight, one of the cofounders of NIKE, says that our entrepreneurial world "breeds an ethic of never giving up, never quitting, when in fact quitting can be pure genius." (from his book, *Shoe Dog*)

These lessons are not easy to learn, especially for people like me who are so achievement-driven. But on that day on the mountain, I didn't question Kristen's decision. And I'm glad I didn't.

Because I might not be writing this.

Of course, I am going back to climb the mountain again. I don't give up easily. Whether or not I succeed on my next climb, I know one thing for sure: I will learn from the experience. I will be grateful to share the experience with amazing people from all over the world, and for the precious gifts I will learn there.

And, as I noted earlier, the summit is not the goal. Each seven days on the mountain is an intense microcosm of my whole life!

It's the journey that teaches you to become a better person. A better leader.

That's what this book is intended to do. To teach you the amazing lessons that will allow you to get your teams, families, and especially YOURSELF to reach whatever summits, dreams, and goals you desire.

I call it the Summit Leadership Model.

The first question I will ask you is, "What kind of leader are you?"

Are you ready to take on the challenge?

**To learn more about the actual
Mountain Leadership Experience**

THE MOUNTAIN
LEADERSHIP EXPERIENCE

Visit: https://www.mountainleadershipexperience.com

Chapter Two

What Kind of Leader Are You?

(Or Do You Choose to Be?)

*"Leadership is not about titles, positions, or flowcharts.
It is about one life influencing another."*

—John C. Maxwell

The Summit Leadership Model works like this. We start at the base of the mountain with our overarching mission—in the simplest of terms, our goal or summit. While we are at the base, we are defining our WHY, getting clear on our values and the values of the team, setting our rules and our code of honor, recruiting the best team members, and above all, training and preparing for the climb.

It is only after all these things are done, that we finally begin our execution, our journey to the summit. Some people like to rush through these steps, taking shortcuts, anxious to reach their goal. Ben and I were a bit like this on our first climb. We didn't have enough time to adequately prepare for a hike as challenging as Kilimanjaro. And we didn't make it.

As a leader, it's your job to make sure that you and your team are fully prepared, motivated, and inspired to reach the summit, whatever that might be. So, I ask, what kind of leader are you?

Most people, when asked what kind of leader they are, immediately consider if they are "good" or "bad" leaders. Those aren't the two categories that come to mind for me when I think about leaders, however. A good leader can have a bad day, week, or year. A bad leader can have a lucky streak and shine their way to the top... for the moment.

Some folks call themselves leaders if they have profile, persona, charisma, and inspiration, but they have no real team. They have admirers or even worshipers, but not folks who will make sacrifices and accept challenges. You'll find these leaders in the world of social media and YouTube.

There are others who perhaps have none of the above, but have a loyal, committed following of team members who would go to the ends of the earth to achieve a mission.

This book is about this last group. Why? Because I am not that charismatic and not that smart. But what I observed on Kilimanjaro I can emulate. In looking at my life, any great thing I have ever done or any nasty predicament I got myself out of, was due to the team I had... not just me.

Let's talk about teams for a moment, because today's definition of a team may be different than it used to be. A team is a group of people who come together for a common purpose and mission. They play by a common set of rules and procedures to make that mission happen. They may dress a certain way, speak a certain way, and have a core set of values. Some of the team may be on the payroll and some may be volunteers. For example, in my organization some of our best salespeople are our customers who have become part of our team.

As an entrepreneur, you start by building a community out in the world, to a large extent through social media, by sharing what you're trying to do, who you are, and why you are doing it. Some of the people in that community will ultimately become your customers. They'll buy from you. And then a subset of those customers might become a part of your team. And what does that mean?

Well, some of them might want to sell for you. Some of them might want to create intellectual property with you or do joint ventures with you. They are a part of your team, yet, none of them are on the payroll. They could be on commission or receive affiliate payouts. Regardless, they still play by the rules when they're dealing with you. They respect the mission and abide by the Code of Honor, and that's what holds them together as a part of the team. It's not the money—it's the mission, the code, and the purpose behind what you are doing that makes a team. They are a team because at some level they feel like part of something bigger than themselves. They feel that by accepting the challenges laid forth by you they will experience the best version of themselves.

Just like on Kilimanjaro. None of us were paid to hike the mountain; we paid for, and had to qualify for, the experience. So the lessons learned on the mountain are that much stronger because they are designed to work best with individuals who have chosen to be there.

People have amazing abilities when put in the right context or environment and given the tools to figure out their way ahead. This is what our guides Kevin and Kristen were great at. They created a context (the climb) without workshops, preaching, snappy slogans, books, podcasts, or seminars that not only transformed all of us on the expedition but became instrumental in transforming Tanzania.

I told you a bit earlier about Kristen, now let me tell you about Kevin, our other guide and leader on these expeditions. Kevin grew up in a tough Italian family in the hard steel town of Pittsburgh, Pennsylvania. His grandfather was the epitome of resilience, having lost his leg after being run over by a train as a boy. It never kept him down; he operated on a peg leg the rest of his life.

In fact, it was Kevin's grandfather who inspired him to see every challenge as an adventure and every goal as possible. He told Kevin there are three types of people—quitters who never start, campers who just stay put, and climbers who take on adventure and risk.

After a rough first year in college, which included a broken back playing basketball, Kevin traveled west to spend some time with a friend and took on the challenge of climbing Mt. Hood in Oregon. This first climb in 1988 opened his eyes to a new type of team sport that invigorated every cell in his body. He was hooked. He was now a climber.

Kevin is a true mountaineer. Although not tall (he's about five foot eight), he has a rough, tough voice that will make you listen and inspire you to dig deeper. I believe he is part man and part mountain goat. His ability to operate at high altitudes is legendary. He's been up Kilimanjaro over fifty times. He has summited Mount Everest and nearly every other major summit in the world. He is a recognized climbing authority in Nepal, Peru, and, of course, Tanzania. In addition to his climbing career, he was a schoolteacher in Scottsdale where the lessons of the mountains inspired his students to be the best they could be. Today his non-profit work and turning others on to the magic of the mountains is his full-time love.

Kevin and Kristen are prime examples of what leaders can do when they choose the right environment for themselves and pursue goals that change lives.

If you are a business owner, parent, coach, or anyone who leads a group to a goal, and you have chosen to lead, I think it's important to do a gut check. What kind of leader do you want to be? Commonly in business I see two categories, both of which are strong and powerful leaders.

The first is:

Wonder Woman

She is legendary. She is fearless, strong, powerful, can dodge bullets and bombs. Others look on in wonder as she races across the battlefield, bombs bursting and bullets flying (ever have a day like that?). The troops are inspired by her and may even be motivated to join the charge. She is a performance leader in that her performance inspires others.

The second is:

Princess Leia

Leia is a very different kind of leader. She has no special super powers or flashy gear. Yet, which of the two does the enemy fear the most?

Leia, because she has something that Wonder Woman does not. She has the Rebellion; a team of fighters from across the galaxy who have banded together to take on the Empire. Her power is in building a team or a coalition. Her power is getting others to take responsibility and raise their games to further the collective mission.

Both styles can be effective. However, Wonder Woman would not get you up Kilimanjaro unless she carried you there (which she could do).

Where in your life are you attempting to be Wonder Woman, Superman, or some equivalent? In other words, where are you trying to lead by being the best and out-performing everyone else? Maybe you're incredibly accomplished, hitting all your goals, and the others will be inspired by you to be better. Hopefully, they will catch up to you. Rather than truly inspiring, they may put their energy into finding ways they can get it done.

If you want to spread a message and get your ideas out to the world, you can do it this way. However, when it comes time to accomplish a mission bigger than you, one that requires the help of others, I am going to say that Princess Leia's leadership is a better, albeit more difficult model. Better because it has depth, substance, and girth. Difficult because it means driving a team of people toward a common goal.

Divider or Unifier?

My friend Robert Kiyosaki identifies two other types of leaders. When it comes to leadership, are you a divider or a unifier? The concept of *divide et impera* (Latin for 'divide and rule') was first used by Julius Caesar as a strategy for conquering the Gauls. It is a reference to stirring up dissension within the ranks of your enemies to make it easier to conquer them, and then to keep them conquered by keeping them divided. Notice that the policy was to divide your 'enemies.' As a military practice, a leader would keep his own troops united.

For these two types of leaders, we think of Caesar and the legendary Attila the Hun, leader of the tribal empire in Central and Eastern Europe in the early fourth century and considered to be one of the most powerful rulers in world history.

Julius Caesar

As a rule, it is much easier to divide, cast doubt, separate, and pit groups against one another. It's much more difficult to unite people towards a common goal. Think of the challenges faced by Abraham Lincoln, Martin Luther King, and JFK.

The most vocal and visible, in-your-face examples of leadership today are politicians. In recent years, they seem to have relied on this concept of divide and conquer. The more they can get the opposing party to fight amongst themselves, the easier it is to win reelection or get a bill passed. But they don't limit the division to just the opposing party. They opt for division within their ranks. Somewhere along the way, the idea of unity has gotten lost in the modern interpretation.

Attila the Hun

I'm not saying divide and conquer isn't a powerful leadership strategy. But when it comes to our businesses, our families, our communities and our lives, the world expects and demands better. Unfortunately, uniting is much, much more difficult to do.

Uniting is what Princess Leia does. It's what great leaders like Martin Luther King and John F. Kennedy did. It's about creating a shared vision and inspiring people to accomplish it with you. It's about leading people to talk with each other, to feel free to express their opinions for the good of the group without fear of repercussion. Breaking down silos and unifying an organization behind a common mission should be a leader's highest priority.

In the popular book, *Radical Candor*, Kim Scott relates a story about Andy Grove, CEO of Intel, talking about Steve Jobs. (I'm paraphrasing here.) "Steve Jobs always gets it right. That doesn't mean he IS right. It means he gets the situation right, and the reason is that he's adamant about people telling him the truth and giving him feedback that he actually can use."

Another thing Scott says about Apple, at least when Jobs was there, is that people had specific functions but they didn't have silos. Someone may have been working on the glass of the iPhone, someone else may have focused on the appearance of the screen, and someone else on the overall design, but they all somehow worked together as well.

To be a leader who unifies requires a level of courage—being open to listening to what the team has to say, even when it may fly in the face of what you believe to be true. In your day-to-day, are you bringing people together or are you dividing them? Are you avoiding an inconvenient truth, discussing it individually with people, and talking about others when they aren't around? Do you perpetuate a mindset of abundance? Do you expect solutions to come about through honest and open communication among the team and collaboration? Bringing a team together when there is confrontation is tough, particularly if you haven't learned how to do it. Some people may not like you in the process.

Teams are not happy camps—most times they are a royal pain in the ass. That's why the average size of an entrepreneurial company is three people. The more people you add, the more complexities, the more differences of opinion, and the more difficult it is to keep them together. But a true sign of a high-performance team is they are willing to air it all out, embrace the differences, and not take it too personally.

Years ago, I had an air freight trucking business with about thirty people. We were in crisis after crisis. There was a lot of arguing and teeth-gnashing, and "No, we can't do this, we can't do that." But at the end of the day, we got it all done. We ended up pulling off miracle after miracle. Because we were unified as a team.

One of the secrets to our unifying success was a technique I called "parking lot conversations." When someone got really heated and upset with someone else, they weren't allowed to bring that attitude into the workplace. They had to go outside to the parking lot with whomever they needed to talk with and work it out. I had two chairs set up by the dumpster on the far edge of the parking lot for these conversations. In them, you told the truth, you went back and forth, and back and forth until some type of resolution was reached.

It's different in my training business. I have trainers all over the world, which makes a parking lot conversation more difficult, even with the advent of Zoom. There's just nothing quite as effective as a face-to-face conversation. And I've found in this training/coaching business that people's skins are pretty thin. They don't like confrontation. So, when I confront someone about something, they get personally very upset, or when someone confronts me, even though I know better, I get personally upset, and it just kills productivity.

That's when I have to step back and remind myself who I am as a leader. Can I keep my ego out of the fight and be able to really listen and trust that at the end of the day, everybody wants to make things work? Can I be a unifier?

You'll learn later that one of our values on Kilimanjaro and in my training academy is that we operate as One Team.

There was a gentleman from Mexico, an entrepreneur and an attorney who came into our organization many years ago. I had to kick him out twice because he couldn't keep his word, he lied, and did all kinds of crazy things. The guy just couldn't play by the rules. He thought taking advantage of other people was a badge of honor. He was a divider.

He aspired to be something better and bigger than himself. He wanted to embody a code of honor, so I took him back once more and he brought a team to Kilimanjaro. During that climb, which I'll talk about it detail later, I, and others, modeled the behavior of a unifying leader. He finally got the message. That climb transformed him into a great leader. His organization has since grown tremendously. He has a livestream broadcast that reaches millions of people across Mexico. He has a training organization with me and stands on some of the largest stages in the world.

Our job as unifying leaders is not to be the person in the middle who creates emotional problems. Often, as leaders, we are unaware of the extent to which our words and actions contribute to a divided organization. Our job is to teach our teams, and ourselves, how to be honest and forthright, to speak passionately about what is bothering us, and still arrive at a resolution. If we can't teach this, then the issue never gets resolved, the divide remains in place, and forever you're just trying to work around the elephant in the room.

Taking it personally, letting it hurt, and not being able to get past it is what keeps teams stuck. Then everybody is walking on eggshells to try and make sure everyone feels okay about this, that, and the other thing.

Amir Ghannad, the author of *The Transformative Leader,* said, "When it comes to leadership, the hard stuff is easy. The soft stuff is hard."

Leadership Style

You'll hear many people say that leaders aren't born, they're made. Generally, I agree with this statement. Yet, most of us are born with, or at least molded into, a propensity for a certain style of leadership. It's a reflection of our personality.

If you research, you'll find articles and books written on anything from three to ten top leadership styles. But from what I've seen, there are four that tend to make every list: The Dictator, The Dealer, The Diplomat, and the Transformer. Let's take a brief look at each one.

The Dictator leadership style is basically my way or the highway. You play by my rules or you don't play. Rules are important, no argument there. Advantage: Get stuff done! Challenge: Others don't like to confront you and withhold the truth. You end up missing critical feedback. On Kilimanjaro, rules were what kept us safe. Rules can keep your business safe too, but if the rules are too strict, or they are the wrong rules, creativity and innovation can be stifled.

The Dealer makes deals to keep the peace and to get things done. You scratch my back and I'll scratch yours. To the Dealer, everyone has an agenda and a self-interest and the way to get a team to function is by somehow satisfying those self-interests. In order to do that, the Dealer creates deals that compensate members for their compliance in exchange for their cooperation in other areas. "I'll let you miss a few sales meetings as long as you maintain certain sales volumes." In other words, I'll give you this and in return, you'll give me that. Advantage: Lots of interaction and catering of needs. Challenge: Creates favorites, separates team members into cliques, and instills a bit of chaos.

The Diplomat style emphasizes working together by everyone agreeing, cooperating, and getting along. Decisions tend to be by consensus and it's critical for everyone to agree. You can get a lot of buy-in with this leadership style, but it often slows things down when the team can't quickly agree. Advantage: Ultimately getting lots of agreements and peace in the group, well liked and respected. Challenge: Slow process to ultimately get all members to engage, agree, and step up. Many are not qualified to make certain decisions or have lots of input due to lack of skills or experience. Kilimanjaro doesn't lend itself to this style. When you only have seven days to get up and down the mountain, and you need to do it safely, there isn't time to debate how it will be done.

A Transformational leadership style, as its name implies, seeks to shift behaviors by inspiring team members to step up to a bigger version of themselves or to focus more on the mission first, then the needs of the team second and individual third. The Transformational leader gets people to be more than they thought they could be. Advantage: Loyal and highly committed team members who will sacrifice momentary ease for long-term mission success. Challenge: Inspiring others takes skill, honesty, experience, and a strange combination of toughness, empathy, and passion.

Any of these leadership styles can work. The most effective leaders are familiar with all of them and know when to adjust their leadership style based on the situation at hand. But in my opinion, the truly great leaders, the ones who not only want success for themselves but for everyone around them, are those who chose to be Transformational leaders.

This is particularly true for entrepreneurs who are competing with major corporations that have deep pockets for talent. Gone are the days when you were the person doing the interviewing and making the decision to hire. Today, a great candidate is interviewing you as well and deciding to work with you or not. "Why would I want to be on your team?" This is a tough question sometimes. It's not only about the money. Your ability to inspire, to show individuals how they can be a part of something so much bigger than themselves, is what will allow you to attract a 'dream team.'

Princess Leia is a Transformational leader. She didn't promise fame or fortune. She promised if you followed her on the journey to overthrow the Empire, your life, and the lives of all you love, would be better.

Kilimanjaro revealed a process of Transformational leadership that took ordinary people from around the world, turned them into a team, got them all safely to the top of one of the largest mountains in the world, and brought them all home in one piece. K2's leadership was concise, powerful, and effective.

While on the mountain, I kept thinking, *if I could apply these principles and techniques to my business and my life, the success would be amazing.*

As a Transformational leader, what are the steps to building a great team? How do you methodically take on and achieve a big goal that is fraught with danger and requires hard work with a group that may have mediocre skills?

As a longtime student of leadership, I have studied great leaders, worked with great leaders, been challenged by great leaders. And to this day, I still ask, what makes a person a great inspirational leader?

What I have decided is that it has to do with something about the "beingness" of the leader. Tom Spooner, a retired Delta operator in the U.S. Army who has completed 10 tours of Afghanistan offered clarity. We agree that to lead requires courage. But what is courage? Certainly courage is confronting your boss about an uncomfortable situation, but when I asked Tom the question he questioned why I was asking it. I told him that I have often wondered what I might do if put under enemy fire. Would I run? Would I hide? Would I freeze? He smiled and said, "Courage is not bravado. Courage is when you are scared out of you mind, at the end of your rope and you take the next step forward anyway." Wow!

I still wasn't sure. In a leadership program I conducted, with Tom in attendance, I was coaching a young woman in the front of the room to keep pushing into her power as she modeled a famous Martin Luther King, Jr. speech. With her body shaking, tears streaming from her eyes, she kept going. Tom reached over to me and quietly said, "You see that, Blair? That is courage!"

Over the next several months I did more trainings with this group and in one of those trainings I was asked to get onto the Jujitsu mat and physically fight — having never fought in my life. That experience changed my life. Being so pummeled, exhausted, and unable to even lift my arms or move my legs... something inside kept me going.

When on Kilimanjaro, all bodily, mental, and emotional strength disappears. Some people quit, but for a few others, something else kicks in. Perhaps it is spirit. Or, as Tom said, courage. Kilimanjaro is an experience that few people in life actually experience. Those people who have faced that brink, that horror, that complete physical breakdown...and kept going, understand a limitlessness that they don't ever need to talk about, but you sense something different about their beingness. In their own style they are transformational, because they have lived the process. We follow them and somehow believe in a greatness in ourselves that we have not yet experienced.

Perhaps that is why the Mountain Leadership Experience is so powerful. It takes ordinary people and puts them onto that transformational line. That is why EVERY person who goes, comes back a bigger and better leader. Not because of what they learn, but because of who they become.

Chapter Three

Mission

"We choose to go to the moon in this decade and do the other things, not because they are easy, but because they are hard. Because that goal will serve to organize and measure the best of our energies and skills."

—John F. Kennedy

How BIG is your game?

For some people, it's getting up in the morning, getting through their to-do list, and going to bed. They do this day after day. That's their game; it's a base level, low-risk, comfortable routine.

Well, answer me this: How big is your game? Is your game big enough to lead you and your team to their own transformations?

Others like to play bigger. They jump out of bed in the morning with a goal or mission in mind that can't be accomplished in a day. It may be risky and is anything but comfortable, but it is exciting. The game stretches their personal development and keeps them going.

Here's an example. I like to keep in shape. I work out pretty regularly. That's my game, my comfortable routine. But when I decided to climb Kilimanjaro, particularly the second time, my game changed. I was on a mission to reach the summit. I didn't stick to my regular routine. I had to up my workouts and train harder because I knew the altitude of Kili would kick my butt if I weren't in tip-top shape. My game got BIGGER.

So, when I ask how BIG is your game, I'm really asking you how BIG is your mission? If your mission is big enough, it will not only inspire you but it will inspire others to become more of who they always hoped they could be.

Kilimanjaro is easy in a way. The goal or the mission is very simple and clear: Get the whole team to the top of the mountain and back safely. It is simple and it's BIG.

But it's also hard. Getting to the summit is only part of the BIG mission for K2. The larger mission is to support disabled and disenfranchised children and families around the world by providing healthcare and education from the proceeds of the climbs and charitable fundraising.

My personal mission in taking driven and positive people, mostly entrepreneurs, up the mountain is to have them experience the biggest, best version of themselves and prioritize their leadership styles. For seven days they are totally unplugged from their business and the world (no cell phone reception), doing hard things mentally and physically, and learning about themselves.

To inspire others to join you on your journey, whatever that might be, you must have a BIG mission. And don't let that scare you. Big doesn't necessarily mean hundreds of thousands of people, global reach, and massive resources. Big is anything that exceeds the current box you live in. Anything that creates a bit of tension between where you are in your life or your business and where you would like to be beyond that. What most people fail to understand is that a big mission challenges them to attain goals they wouldn't otherwise attain. Maybe you don't hit the ultimate goal. But I can guarantee you've gotten bigger. You've had more of an impact on yourself, on your team, and on your community than you would have had if you simply played small. You haven't failed in not reaching the ultimate goal because you moved forward, you made progress. You need to celebrate those wins.

THE GOAL IS NOT IT! I'll talk more about this later, but on Kili, it's not about the summit. If you are only focused on the summit and something happens and you can't make it, you will view the whole thing as a failure. However, if every step is a win, every day is a win, and you are 100% in the moment, there is no way to lose. All there is, is a series of ever-increasing wins.

The Little Voice Saboteur

Often we decide not to play big because our "Little Voice" says no. You know the "Little Voice" I'm talking about. It's the one in your head that just said, "What 'Little Voice?'" We all have them. They whisper things like: you're not good enough, smart enough, skinny enough; what will people think; what if you fail; you're a loser; nobody is going to listen to you; what if, what if, what if? Learning how to manage those little voices, particularly when they don't serve you, is crucial to being successful in all areas of your life.

I talk about silencing the "Little Voice" in detail in my book *Little Voice Mastery: How to Win the War Between Your Ears in Thirty Seconds or Less*. For the majority of us, the path to success is the distance between our right ear and our left ear—the battleground in our brains. Most people listen to the incessant conversation going on in their minds and they believe everything they hear. Without going into detail right here, all that conversation is not necessarily the real you. It is the composite of your parents, teachers, preachers, media, politicians, friends, and a myriad of old experiences. The minute you are able step outside yourself and look at yourself objectively and observe the conversation from a distance is when little voice mastery starts.

Once you become conscious of your Little Voice, you can control it. You can turn those negative what-ifs into positives. You see, the minute you imagine a bigger goal, a larger mission, or accomplishing something beyond your current routine, the Little Voice kicks in. "Who do you think you are? You can't do that. You will look like a fool. No one will believe you. You aren't smart enough. You don't have the resources. It's a fool's dream. Those things are reserved for bigger, better people than you..." Sound familiar? The good news is that most everyone has those Little Voice thoughts. Courage is taking the next step anyway. The moment you do, the world begins to unfold in a different, sometimes mysterious way. At the minimum you will grow exponentially. At the maximum, you may attract amazing people whom you might never have encountered had you stayed small. You can allow yourself to have a big mission.

A Powerful Recruiting Tool

Based on the above, it may seem obvious that creating a strong mission would be the first step to putting a team together. However, early in my career, while I knew mission was important, I did not give it much credence. I just wanted my companies to be the best and make a lot of money. Sound familiar?

Yet, in each case, as we grew and started making more money, the individual companies began to show signs of weakening. Why? Because it became clear we weren't all on the same page in terms of mission. There were multiple agendas in play. Different people wanted different things. Some wanted money, some wanted fame, some wanted to just get by.

I found, to my amazement, that people had joined us and were a part of what we were doing for very different reasons. We couldn't even provide what some of them wanted. This diversity of goals, of mission, would create divides, separate camps, and ultimately a tear down the middle of the organization.

My first big business was the air freight trucking operation I mentioned earlier in this book. It was based out of Los Angeles, California. I had two partners in this business and we divided our responsibilities along with our strengths. Mine was sales and marketing, another's was logistics, and the third partner's was finance. We seemed to work well together when we started but we really had no mission other than building a money-making trucking operation. As the business began to take off, our partnership began to falter.

My reason for building the business was I wanted to prove to myself I could build a business of this size. I wanted to create a source of passive income so I could follow my true passion, which was to teach others how to be entrepreneurial leaders. Building the business and the resultant cash flow would be proof to me that I could make something like that happen.

The partner who was in charge of logistics wanted to build the business for his own prestige and to impress his friends. He wanted to make a big name for himself in the air freight industry and for another reason, which

I'll explain in a bit. The partner in charge of finance simply felt building the business would be a good financial opportunity.

Now, it would seem that those three reasons line up. But when problems started to hit the fan, when things started to go wrong, (which they invariably do) when we had a few growth challenges, when clients stopped paying us or went out of business... the three of us reverted to our individual goals and stopped thinking about the good of the company.

The finance partner bailed first. He said, "There's no money in this, it's too hard to make money. I'm out." That left me and the logistics partner to slave away, working to keep the company afloat. Then my partner decided we should open a branch office in San Francisco, even though it would drain the remaining funds out of the organization. He went up there every weekend, supposedly to ensure things were operating well.

A few months later, I was coming back from a trip and landed in San Francisco, so I thought I'd stop by the terminal on a Friday night. My partner wasn't there. And when I asked the team where he was, they said they hadn't seen him for weeks. It turned out, even though he was married and had three beautiful children, he had a girlfriend in San Francisco. The terminal gave him a perfect excuse to see her every weekend. Needless to say, he had to leave our organization because his mission was not aligned with the mission of building an air freight trucking operation.

At the end of the day, the trucking operation, although it had its moments of success, ultimately failed. Why? Because leadership was not on the same page. Whatever success the company did have was in large part due to our team. They were mostly Samoan, Tongan, Mexican, and African-American workers. They had a mission. Their mission was to operate as a team, work together, and take on any challenge that came across the warehouse floor. And you know what? Despite poor leadership and poor management on our part, they did it every single time. They rescued the company from the brink of disaster more than once!

I learned a big lesson from this team of hardworking, we're-going-to-get-it-done individuals. I learned that the mission needs to be clear from the top to the bottom. In this case, the mission of the team was stronger than the agendas of the leadership. It's no wonder something had to give.

How was I fortunate to attract such an amazing team in spite of my ineptitude? I'll cover that in the next chapter.

Obviously, a simple clear mission is step one. It keeps everyone aligned and focused. Yet, it wasn't until a conversation I had with current Congressman, Jack Bergman, who was retired from the Marine Corps, that I fully grasped the importance of mission. During part of his career, Jack was in charge of Marine Corps recruiting. I asked him, "How do you recruit 18 to 25 year olds, put them in harm's way, pay them very little, work them to the bone, and have them be so loyal?"

He said it was not that difficult. He said the Marine Corps figured out people of that age want to be part of something bigger than themselves. Something that is solid, that they can believe in, that won't change its mind. They are also willing to go through a journey that has the promise of helping them become someone bigger and better.

Does your organization do that?

Kilimanjaro makes its mission crystal clear. The question each climber asks months before the climb is, "What kind of a person will I have to become to get to the top of that mountain?"

It is a tradition to take your country's flag or your business's banner to the summit to display for the rest of the world to see in your photos and videos. The pride in accomplishing the climb is definitely worth celebrating. That you, as a representative of your group, achieved the summit is monumental.

Yet, for everyone on our team, there was something else propelling them. When you experience the early morning steam rising off the rocks and crags of the mountain, when you see ice crystals strewn on the ground like piles of precious diamonds, when you see a massive glacier glistening like a crown jewel in the sun, you get a sense of belonging to something much bigger than just your business.

I'm going to go into depth about the importance of recruiting the right team in a later chapter. But for now, understand this. Your mission becomes your most powerful recruiting tool.

Let's say you are interviewing two people and you ask them why they want to work with you. (By the way, this is true for contractors and potential team members alike.)

One says, "I think I can fit in here."

The other says, "I really want to be part of something bigger than me, and it seems if I work here, I am going to get pushed to greater levels."

The second candidate is willing to play bigger. They understand and relate to the mission. They are not looking to simply make money or fit in, but to have an impact on the company and the world around them. They aren't looking to throw a pebble into a stream to see how far the ripples go. They want to toss a cinder block in and create a tidal wave.

Which one do you want?

When you lead with mission, you attract candidates who aren't satisfied with the status quo, with being mediocre. At the end of the day, you want everyone working with you for the right and similar reasons.

SIGNIFICANCE

Not everyone needs to set out to change the world. A big mission for a solopreneur may be to take their product global via social media. For a parent it may be to raise a group of rambunctious kids into great human beings who make a difference in the world. It may be a commitment to make your team into the most amazing team in your industry.

Big does not necessarily mean volume or dollars or breadth. For me, it simply needs to attempt, as Steve Jobs once said, to "make a dent in the universe." ...in your own way. Be inspired by great goals, but don't be intimidated by them.

What's Your Big Mission?

I'm sure most of you are familiar with the concept of a mission statement. But just to ensure we're all on the same page, let's talk briefly about the key components of a strong mission.

Simply put, a mission statement is a short statement about **what** you do, **why** your company exists, and the **values** you hold dear. It's a summary of what your business does and why you do it stated in a way that highlights the values that are important to you.

Your WHY describes the spark, the passion behind your business. Your values describe the worth you provide and the principles by which you operate.

The mission of Blair Singer Training Academy is to improve the quality of life for everyone by producing the best teachers, leaders, and facilitators in the world who help entrepreneurs succeed. Our WHAT is to create great teachers who help entrepreneurs succeed. Our WHY is to improve the quality of life for everyone. Our value is to be and create the best in the world. We won't settle for mediocrity. Those who love to teach, love to learn, and love entrepreneurship are attracted. Those who don't are not.

Starbucks' mission reads, *"to inspire and nurture the human spirit— one person, one cup, and one neighborhood at a time."* Their WHY is to inspire and nurture. Intrinsically, their value is to raise up humanity.

Microsoft has this mission, *"to empower every person and every organization on the planet to achieve more."* Their WHY overall is to make the world a better place. They'll achieve this by believing that every product they create actually empowers others.

Your big mission is the glue that holds your team together, that allows them to perform in unison to reach common goals, which are the milestones to attaining the mission. I can't stress enough the significance of being ONE team. This concept of One Team was probably the most powerful lesson I, and others, learned going up the mountain.

On our second Mountain Leadership Experience trip, I was taking a team comprised of amazing individuals from six different countries. One young woman from Russia and an older gentleman from Mexico spoke no

English. Of the group of seventeen (not counting our guides and myself), eight were from Mexico. Within the group from Mexico, there were two smaller groups who had been brought by their leaders. By the time we reached the second camp, it was apparent that the Mexican contingent was having a great time: joking, singing, laughing, but mostly in Spanish, and mostly between themselves. I could see the others were distancing themselves from this group because they did not understand Spanish. The non-Spanish speakers were feeling isolated and began to complain about not being included. Some even wondered if the Mexican team was laughing about them.

During this climb, it rained hard for the second and third days. So hard the trails were turning into small streams. Everyone's gear was getting soaked. Morale was at an all-time low. On the evening of day three, the rain had turned to ice. We were all cold and wet.

As we opened our debrief of the day, with the wind whipping our meal tent, I listened to the shallowness of their comments on the day with their underlying tones of unhappiness. I interrupted the discussion and yelled out above the wind to the group, "We are taking ONE TEAM to the top of this mountain." Except for the driving rain and wind outside, everything went deadly silent.

I explained what was happening. Not surprisingly, the Mexican contingent got defensive and claimed they were not excluding. Yet, other team members shared their desire to be one team as well and felt it was not going that way.

At that moment, the conversation could have gone the wrong way. If allowed to be defensive on one side or victimized on the other, it would have created a giant wedge within the team. This happens all the time in business. I emphasized that I did NOT say to not have fun, to not speak Spanish, to not enjoy your friends. I repeated, "We are taking ONE TEAM to the top. Not a Mexican team, not an Asian team, not an American team."

I said, "You are all leaders in this tent. I have one goal for this group. That by the time we reach the summit of this mountain, I want you all to fall in love with each other...all of you!"

It was a strange comment and an even stranger goal, but it popped out of my mouth as if the mountain made me say it. I told them I was not going to tell them how to do it, but they needed to figure it out. There was silence for a moment in the tent. Everyone looked deep inside.

Then there was agreement, there were some high fives and hugs, and all I know is from that moment on everything about the team dynamic changed. Even the weather cooperated. The next morning was stunning, although still cold. The ground was strewn with dazzling diamond-like shards of ice. It was as if the mountain had forced the nasty weather on us to teach us a lesson. By the time we all reached the summit, this group was so in love that even weeks later they were still sharing, texting, and planning together.

Russians were talking with Mexicans even though they did not understand the languages. The two teenagers in the group became gurus and great leaders. It was probably the most tightly bonded team I have seen in many years. It was an honor to facilitate. The 100% summit success rate of the team was absolutely a result of the shift they all made at the third camp. The shift to working under a common goal—not the mission to reach the summit, but the goal to honor, respect, and love one another on the journey—ensured the ultimate success of the journey and provided a big lesson.

The greatest goals a team can set are the ones that define what kind of a team they want to be. Certainly, the summit is the magnet that pulls us all along and gives us the motion, but I think it's the desire to BE who we want to BE and help each other get there, that creates the magic.

Although a mission statement is short, it doesn't mean crafting one is easy, particularly if you want the impact to be big. Big enough to bring the right team to your cause. Rarely is the first draft where your passion resides. It requires deep thought. It requires peeling back the onion one layer at a time until you have crystal clarity around your WHY and your values.

So, let's get started peeling. What's your WHY?

Chapter Four

Why?

"*There is no greater gift you can give or receive than to honor your calling. It's why you were born.*"

—*Oprah Winfrey*

Remember in the last chapter I said the goal is not it? I'm sure you started scratching your head thinking, *Blair, the goal has to be it, otherwise, why would you have one?*

Yes, why in the world would I train for months, travel all the way to Tanzania to climb a mountain I had barely heard of, deal with cold, wet, altitude, and sleeping in a little tent, particularly when I am not even a big fan of hiking?! Give me a sunset on the beach, crystal clear tropical lagoons, and a steady trade wind. Now THAT is a vacation!

It's because climbing Kilimanjaro was never about summiting a mountain. It was about doing community service and taking an adventure with my then 16-year-old son, Ben. It happened because a couple of weeks after the decision to do community service, I "happened" to be sitting on a plane and "happened" to talk to a total stranger sitting next to me about community service events. (And get this, in all my countless air miles, I NEVER talk to people sitting next to me on planes.) He "happened" to mention these friends of his who do this amazing community service in Africa, and that they "happened" to climb this mountain.

Why do I keep saying "happened"? It's because when you pick the 'right' goals for the seemingly 'right' reasons, magic seems to occur as if the universe were laying out the path for you. Let me explain.

If you are going to set a goal of any size or magnitude, there will be adversity. There will be challenges. And when the going gets rough, you better have a good reason why you're doing this or you will quit.

Have you ever said to yourself in the middle of a disaster, "This seemed like a good idea at the time!" Building a business is a great 'idea.' However, most businesses fail and not because they don't have a decent business idea or plan. It's because once you step onto the entrepreneurial playing field, you're going to get knocked down. More than a few times. After enough knocks the 'Little Voice' in your head starts to entertain doubts and fears. If you do not have a compelling reason WHY you are doing what you do, those doubts and fears can win. And many times in business, money is not enough of a reason.

Oftentimes, particularly if you are working for someone else, the goals you have to set may seem meaningless to you or your team. Great leaders are those who can attach great meaning to things that seem meaningless. "Why do we have to put in all these hours on a project that the company may not even support in the future? It doesn't put any more money in our pockets."

As a leader, this becomes your moment of truth. This is when you ask yourself the tough questions. What kind of a team would we have to become in order to pull this off? How strong, how committed would we need to be? How would the lessons of this experience be invaluable to all of our futures when we go on to lead our own teams?

The answers to those questions will determine the strength of the team.

An anonymous writer once penned, "When you know your WHY, the how is easy." What is left unsaid in this quote, however, is that knowing your WHY can be hard—often, the hardest thing we must do.

Knowing your WHY takes a willingness to look deep, to go beyond the easy answer of "making money" to the very core of what makes your business worthy of customers. It takes uncovering your purpose, your cause, your beliefs, the reasons someone other than you would care. People don't buy what you do, they buy who you are and why you do it.

Once you have determined your mission or goal, it is critical to make a list of all the reasons WHY you want it. I suggest you do this for yourself and have the members of your team do it as well. Take a piece of paper and start listing your Whys. Why do you want to accomplish this goal? Write ten reasons. Then write five more, and again, five more. Somewhere near the end of that list, your real WHY will emerge.

Many people start with I want to make money. Making money may be part of your WHY. But why do you want to make the money? Why is that important? Keep digging.

Simon Sinek, in his book, *Find Your Why*, explains your WHY like this, ". . . a statement of your value at work as much as it is the reason your friends love you. We don't have a professional WHY and a personal WHY. We are who we are wherever we are. Your contribution is not a product or a service. It's the thing around which everything you do—the decisions you make, the tasks you perform, the products you sell—aligns to bring about the impact you envision."

When I work with my teams and coach others, I suggest each person get a bit selfish and ask themselves, "Why do I want to achieve this?" If you dig deep enough into your own mind and tell the truth, you may come up with some powerful answers: To prove to myself I can do it; To become the type of person I want to be; To make all those disbelievers take notice; To make a contribution to others.

These reasons go beyond money and time. They go to the spiritual core of each person and the team itself.

Climbing Kili the second time, I had to keep going to set an example for my son, and also to prove to myself I could do it. I keep going back because Kili always teaches me something I did not expect to learn about myself. Other team members over the years have had varied reasons for going. Several have gone to honor a deceased loved one, spreading their ashes or leaving a specific memento. Some go to leave their pasts behind, to turn a page in their lives....

One member of our team, in particular, went for the physical challenge, which resulted in dramatically changing his life. He was in his sixties, had some heart issues, and was turned back at Stella Point the first time he tried to reach the summit. But he'd experienced enough to know he wanted to conquer this mountain. So, he trained and he trained, and the next year he made it to the summit. His wife was so appreciative. She told me, "Oh my God, you know we had issues with his health and now he's the epitome of health and fitness. You saved his life."

If your reason WHY is not compelling enough, if each morning it doesn't make you thankful for another chance to make a difference, either don't do it or learn to manufacture reasons why you will benefit. And by manufacture, I don't mean lie to yourself about the WHY. I mean dig deeper to find a reason that makes sense.

Sometimes you are faced with something that you MUST do, even if you don't want to do it. As a leader, you have a responsibility, regardless of how distasteful it may be, to create a WHY because opting out is NOT an option. At the end of the day, by manufacturing whys, you will find a TRUE reason why. For example, I will keep fighting for this business because I love this team; I will push past this paralyzing fear because I am an example to my community and family.

There's always a reason behind every worthy goal or mission to which you are introduced. The ones you decide to take on may require you to overcome your normal fears, aversions, delusions, and Little Voice to get to the WHY.

Remember I said that if you set the right goals for the right reasons, magic will happen. The W.H. Murray quote from the *Scottish Himalayan Expedition* comes to mind. "Whatever you can do, or dream you can, begin it. Boldness has power, genius, and magic in it."

Many climbers go with me out of a sense of curiosity and personal challenge—they're just intrigued by the program. As Dr. Jordan B. Peterson, a psychology professor at the University of Toronto and the bestselling author of *12 Rules for Life: An Antidote to Chaos* says, "Some of us are intrigued to adventure." We're intrigued to adventure because there's a certain benefit or a certain amount of risk that gets us pumped.

It's not an adventure if there's no risk, right? On an adventure, there's a suggestion that you're going to have to face a demon somewhere along the way. If you survive the journey, conquer that demon, dragon, or whatever, you're going to be better, you're going to become the mythical hero of your own life.

Since you are reading this book, I know you are on a journey. It could be a journey of business growth, technical growth, income growth, or emotional growth, but for sure it's a journey of personal growth. Your journey is unique to you. It's based on your background, your stories, the environment you have come through, and possibly even your DNA.

It's a 'Hero's Journey.' Joseph Campbell, a literature professor at Sarah Lawrence College and author of *The Hero with a Thousand Faces,* says that throughout human history, many cultures have passed on the 'Hero's Journey.' The story is nearly the same regardless of time, culture, language, or circumstance. It is about a seemingly restless, but common person who gets called upon to take on some great task. They encounter wizards, shamans, enemies, allies, great tests of valor and skill to vanquish an enemy, and, ultimately, return home transformed in the process. Whether it's Dorothy in *The Wizard of Oz*, or Jason going for the Golden Fleece, or Luke Skywalker battling Darth Vadar, it's the same story with a different face.

As humans, we've been attracted to these stories for thousands of years because we see ourselves as the hero. You and I are on a hero's journey of our own. At some level, we have the awareness we could be better, we could be more. Entrepreneurs are perfect examples of individuals who are on a hero's journey as they opt to take risks to reach their WHY; their ultimate goal.

Each goal set is another step toward our transformation. When you are on course, or when your reasons why are even more compelling than the goal itself... when magic in the form of resources, ideas, strength, support, or inspiration appears—sometimes just in the nick of time.

There are not a lot of promises when we bring leaders to Kilimanjaro. There is no promise you will reach the summit. There is no guarantee you won't struggle. But what we do guarantee is you will experience the very best version of yourself on that mountain. And you know what? For most people that is priceless.

One final note—your WHY isn't always static.

Your WHY may evolve and be refined as you grow, add experiences, and change circumstances in life. Sometimes this results in a new focus or direction for you or your existing business, or it could result in shutting down the old and starting something new.

At the beginning of this chapter, I said knowing your WHY requires uncovering your purpose, your cause, and your beliefs. What this really means is uncovering your core values. So, I ask you—what do you value?

Chapter Five

Values

*"One of the keys to life is a person's commitment
to live in harmony with their values."*
—*Mack Newton*

Your business card says owner, CEO, director, founder, president...
does that make you a leader? Are you a leader by election, designation,
appointment, or default? Certainly, you would agree the label does not
necessarily bestow leadership on anyone.

We've heard actions speak louder than words. We have heard congruent
leadership is when thoughts, words, and actions all line up to support
missions and outcomes. One of my great teachers, coaches, and friends is a
7th Degree Black Belt Master Instructor and a two-time world Taekwondo
champion. His name is Mack Newton. He teaches that success is showing
'one face,' meaning what you do, what you think, and what you say must
all be congruent to who you are at a base value level. Otherwise, you are
out of sync, not fully effective, at cross purposes.

Where does that congruence come from? It comes from the
cornerstones of those core values you hold most dear: honor, integrity,
love, family, honesty, health, education, personal growth, loyalty, wealth,
equality, freedom, etc.

Any project or institution of worth, size, or duration is built on
a bedrock of values. According to the online Cambridge Dictionary
English version, *values are the principles that help you decide what is right*

and wrong, and how to act in various situations. Notice the word "act" in this definition. Values are not meant to simply inspire, but to move people to action. Values provide the how; the desired behaviors team members should use in reaching your goals and mission. They are the guiding beliefs on which your company is based. They bring your WHY to life.

It is from these values you begin to build the culture and context that shapes the business or project with which you are involved. Your values must impact all aspects of your business, both internal and external. Internally, your values will determine compensation, rewards, and the policies you put in place. They will also guide the strategic decisions that are made. Externally, your values educate the public about who you are. They set clear expectations for your clients, your partners, and your communities.

The people you attract will be those who feel an affinity for these values, just as two tuning forks vibrate in harmony. They may even be willing to work for a company that pays less because the organization is aligned with their personal values. These values will create rules, which will govern processes, which will attract your teams.

If you ask anyone who has ever climbed with K2 what the guiding team's core values are, they will resoundingly answer with 'safety and health.' Notice these values have little to do with achievement, summiting, strength, or endurance. Yet, they are why the number of people who actually summit the mountain with the K2 team is over 96%, while the average for all climbers is less than 40%. On Kili, the alignment of values can be the difference between summitting or not, enjoying the experience of suffering, and coming down safely or on a gurney.

Another key value on Kilimanjaro is support—no team member left behind. One particular Mountain Leadership Experience group was filled with strong and accomplished entrepreneurs, owners, trainers, and leaders. All people who were used to giving support to others. They were the thought leaders, the focal points, and the go-to people for their organizations. But Kili was determined to teach us a lesson that would change everyone's life. Through the adversity of the trek, nearly every person found themselves in need of support from others—physically, mentally, or emotionally.

One team member from Malaysia was struggling with the climb. His highest climb in the past had been only 5000 feet and even at that altitude, he had gotten very sick. On summit day, I could see he was struggling again, but determined. I slid in behind him for the 45-minute section before we would break. I talked to him the entire time, reminding him to 'rest step' and pressure breathe. I exaggerated my breathing so he could hear it and get into a rhythm. I kept telling him, "You look good, you look strong, you got this." When we got to the next break, I asked him how he felt. He said he was still hurting, but he felt stronger and more confident.

At Stella, the last break before the summit, I gave him a huge hug and congratulated him for an amazing accomplishment, thinking this would be enough for him. An hour later, as I stood at the final summit, to my amazement I saw him trudging toward us. He had made it the entire way. He said there was no way he would have ever come close to summiting that mountain without the continued support, encouragement, and love of the team. It was a lesson nearly everyone learned, and in our debrief we wrote this affirmation, "I now allow others to love and support me."

Instilling the values of safety, health, and support within the group began long before any of us actually set foot on the mountain. In the months leading up to the climb, Kevin and Kristin were teaching us how to train, what to pack and why, the issues we could encounter on the trail, and countless other things. We had to buy in to those values before we could climb.

I used to give lip service to the importance of values in business. I took it semi-seriously. I felt the more success we achieved, the less important it was to focus on value alignment. Boy, was I wrong.

In one of my businesses, we were growing like gangbusters. Millions of dollars were flowing into the organization. As a training franchisor, we had a global reach in over 30 countries and we were gaining power in the market. One of the core values of our business was personal growth and education. Yet, as we grew so did our challenges and problems. I had a partner in the business, and over time it became apparent our definitions of personal growth, education, and wealth management were different.

My definition of personal growth was actively seeking qualified coaching, counseling, and programs to help me evolve and develop. My definition was predicated on taking 100% responsibility for everything in my life. My partner's idea of personal growth was reading books and working on himself without any outside support or coaching. While he verbally agreed to the idea of 100% accountability, our definitions once again differed in action. This showed up in heated arguments, blaming, scolding, and other forms of verbal abuse from both sides.

This slight difference turned into a huge gap. It was like a small hole in a balloon that, while deflated, is unnoticeable. But as you inflate it and fill it with more air, the hole gets bigger...not smaller. You keep trying to fill it, but it keeps leaking out at a faster and faster rate until the whole thing bursts. The result was that a long-term partnership was dissolved. The business went away and all the magic that had gone into its creation faded into the sunset.

So, it's not just the values. It's the understanding of what those values mean in day-to-day operation. Values are crucial for creating a successful business or personal life, but to have meaning they must be proactive. Values may, on some occasions, cost you. By that, I mean strong values will force you to make choices between what is right and what is wrong for your company, even if that means a short-term physical or economic hardship. Values are non-negotiable. What you say no to is just as important as what you say yes to.

Dr. Buckminster Fuller, American architect, inventor, author, design scientist and futurist, always said there is no right or wrong. It either works or it doesn't work. Situations change, environments change. It's easy to get swept away by what other people are doing, and it takes a really strong leader to continually redefine and apply core values in current relevant situations.

In other words, if everybody is jumping on the bandwagon and doing social media blasts, but those social media blasts and the ads don't ring true to what you deliver as a company, then following that trend is going to be a compromise of your values and your business may suffer.

Our organization trains trainers all over the world, and it's very tempting to shortcut the process of getting a trainer to be fully qualified and certified. Yet, we have to resist that temptation. I mean, certainly, it might be more economical and much faster to redesign our system. And we can redesign what we're doing and how we're doing it as long as we don't compromise our values. It's an important consideration. But shortcutting those values would, again, be like sticking a pin in a deflated balloon and creating a little hole. Over time, as you add more air (or money and people) to it, the hole gets much bigger.

We all come together because we share the value of 'teamwork.' Yet, for some, their personal priorities come first. For others, the team comes first. For still others, the mission comes first. Who is right? There is no right. There is only our definition and agreement of what teamwork is.

Try this little exercise. Gather several of your team members together. Ask each one to take thirty seconds to write down their five most important personal core values. Then have each person read their list quickly without commenting on them. Chances are you will have one or more values in common with the group—even if they are phrased slightly different.

That's great! You share similar values. That is what attracted you to one another. Birds of a feather, right?

Now, take the one or two you had most in common and have each person spend no more than ten seconds defining what that common value means to them. I bet you will not get the same definitions. Therein lies the problem.

If the common value was integrity, one person might define it as telling the truth, while another defines it as completing tasks and creating wholeness.

Love for one person may mean compassion and embrace, while for another it could mean ruthless tough love. I am sure you can see the potential conflicts.

Neither definition is better or worse than the other. However, you need to agree on what your values mean for the team so they are pulling together.

Try this exercise at home with your spouse or companion. At a minimum, it will deepen your conversations and understanding of each other, and, hopefully, your relationships.

Defining Your Values

Remember I said I used to give lip service to the importance of values? Well, the same can be said of many companies when they define their values. Take Boeing for example. According to their website, the first value they list is to start with engineering excellence—to build and maintain products with safety, quality, and integrity. Then came the Boeing 737 Max, which had a faulty automated flight control system that resulted in two crashes killing 346 people. Was it the result of management pressing for shortcuts and money-saving solutions against the recommendations of low-level FAA officials and Boeing's own safety experts?

Boeing had a slew of beautiful values that were compromised. It cost lives. Team members become cynical when they feel values are being used as a marketing ploy. Clients become distrustful as well. And in extreme cases, like Boeing's, customers may suffer.

Building your values statement is not about creating a list, it's about purposefully deciding the type of company or person you want to be. The values shouldn't be a wish list of how you want your team to behave, but a declaration of how they actually will behave. Values have to be easy to understand and remember. If your values make you a little bit uncomfortable from time to time because of the choices they force you to make, that's fine.

Take Johnson & Johnson for example and the Tylenol scare of 1982. It wasn't clear how many bottles had been tampered with, but Johnson & Johnson pulled every bottle off the shelves at a significant cost. Why? Because one of their core values was the health and safety of their customers. Despite the negative impact to their sales, they stood by their values and made the right choice for their customers.

You can use the exercise I mentioned above to begin to get a handle on your core values. Here are some additional questions you can ask to get to the crux of your values.

1. What kind of company do we want to be?
2. What do we want to be known for?
3. How will our values set us apart from our competition?
4. What is our passion?
5. What makes people want to work here?
6. What behaviors will and won't be tolerated?
7. What causes people to leave?

And most importantly.......
8. What is the right thing to do?

I could give you examples of some highly regarded companies' value statements, but I won't. What is right for those companies may not be right for your company. Your values are unique to you.

My friends, Josh and Lisa Lannon, are great entrepreneurs and Rich Dad Advisors, who created a very successful drug and alcohol treatment rehab business. They built an organization from the ground up using all of the things I've been or will be talking about—Code of Honor, Mission Statements, and Values. They had an amazing team making millions of dollars and changing hundreds of patients' lives. They ultimately sold the business to a private equity company.

The company that bought the business was looking to expand its reach across America. Even though the company they bought from my friends was hugely successful, as soon as the new owners took over and Josh and Lisa left with their sizable payout, the business began to go south. Within a year, the thriving business was gone because the new owners had abandoned the original values and mission and code. They looked at the business as a group of statistics: dollars and cents and the number of people served. They didn't understand or care about the core values and mission that took to drive it.

Today, Josh and Lisa have built an even bigger business in the same industry servicing first responders and veterans suffering from PTSD and substance abuse called Warrior's Heart. Once again, it is hugely successful because it is based on core values and a strong code of honor that everyone agrees to from the top to the bottom of the organization.

And by the way, if you're going to create a code and you're going to create values, what's good for one is good for all. If we say to be on time, that means the CEO is on time as well. It means everyone is on time for every event because everyone is accountable. Nobody gets special treatment or exceptions. Everybody buys in or nobody buys in. That's how values and a code of honor work together.

Once you have agreed to the values, you must put them into action. Like the training Kevin and Kristin did months before our climb, it is critical you take the time to ensure your teams understand how the values are put into practice. One of the ways to do that is to create the RULES that protect and define those values.

Chapter Six

Code of Honor – The Rules

*"The ultimate measure of a man is not where he stands
in moments of comfort and convenience, but where he stands
at times of challenge and controversy."*

—Martin Luther King Jr.

"Do NOT take any medications on this mountain unless you clear them through me first, particularly if you have never taken them before!"

I have heard Kristen bark that rule hundreds of times. Her knowledge of health, what happens to your body at altitude under stress, and her crystal clarity of what it takes to be safe has saved lives on Kilimanjaro.

Yet, buried in my sleeping bag in the solitude of my tent with the freezing wind howling in the middle of the night, I didn't think. I broke the rule. In order to calm a slightly queasy stomach, I ingested medication I had never taken before and without Kristen's permission. I thought I knew better. I thought her rules were for 'other people' who were not as healthy or as experienced as me!

Later that morning, I paid the price for that breach of the rules at 18,000 feet, and it could have been a lot worse.

The next step, before you recruit your ideal team to set out on your journey, is that the values you have defined must be relegated to a set of rules. We call this sacred set of rules a Code of Honor. It's not a policy manual; not a thirty-page manifesto. It is a simple set of rules by which you and your business navigate through the storms of life.

In my book *Team Code of Honor*, I go into this in a lot of detail: how to create the rules, enforce the rules, and perpetuate the rules. I'll weave some of those concepts into this chapter, but if you really want to understand how a Code of Honor impacts not only your business but everyone around you, I suggest you read the book.

First of all, let's start by defining the terms. According to the online Cambridge Dictionary English version, a code is defined as, *a system of words, letters, or signs which is used to represent a message in secret form, or something in a shorter or more convenient form.* This definition implies that a code is unique, special, and not for everyone. But we're talking about a Code of HONOR.

So, what does Honor mean? Again, according to the Cambridge Dictionary, it means *to do what you promised or agreed to do.*

Another definition I like was given to me by one of my great mentors: *"The correct reciprocation of value and exchange, and delivering what is promised with exact and precise correctness."*

I like this definition because it assumes reciprocation. Not only do you do what you say you will do, but others reciprocate in kind, thus creating an 'honorable exchange' in the relationship.

Not all exchanges are honorable. When you give and somebody doesn't reciprocate, or somebody takes but they don't give, that's called 'criminal exchange.' You may not realize it, but you could be breeding criminal behavior simply by allowing a person to break a rule that you are keeping.

There's also another type of exchange called 'hopeful exchange.' This is when you, as the leader or a team member, commit to playing by the rules. You 'hope' that by other people watching and observing your behavior, they will follow suit. That typically doesn't work because others either shrug off your demonstration or they feel that you are trying to shame them into compliance. Instead of being inspired, they figure, "Well, Mary's working pretty hard. That's just her. Good. She's covering for me."

So, having a Code of Honor, is about having honorable exchange where everybody reciprocates. I play by the rules and you play by the rules. We work together. But let me give you an example of how that goes awry.

We had a marketing team working very hard on social media and YouTube, getting our message out to the world. Certain members of these teams were independent contractors. Regardless, all agreed to be held accountable for certain tasks and getting them done in a certain amount of time.

We had one particular member who was very talented, but she was never able to be accountable. She skipped meetings and missed deadlines. She made promises and didn't keep them. Ultimately, she had to be removed from the team, and the minute she was, the performance of the team improved several levels. This happens a lot.

I worked with a magazine firm in South Africa. The team was in sales, responsible for selling advertisements for the magazine. Their goal was to increase sales. The first thing I did was to help them create a Code of Honor for themselves.

This was a team of about ten people but two of the people were lightyears ahead of everyone else in sales. They were the top producers and accounted for nearly eighty percent of the sales. We created the code of honor with rules that included showing up to meetings, being on time, and being accountable. The top two performers didn't like them. Some people like to live in a gray area so they can make their own rules. The minute it goes black and white they don't like it, and these two top producers were definitely in that camp.

A couple of weeks later, I got a call from their manager. He said, "Look, I have this problem." The two top producers didn't want to abide by the code. "What should I do?"

I told him, "Well if you're going to do this, you're going to have to live by it. You have to live or die by the sword in this case. If you're going to be a leader, you've got to step up and do it. If you don't want to do it, that's fine, but you have to tell the rest of the team you've decided not to go by these rules anymore. You have to make a stand here one way or the other."

To his credit, he took a stand and called the top producers out. They complained that they shouldn't have to come and they didn't need the meetings. He said, "Look, if you're not going to come, if you're not going to play by the rules we agreed to, including you, then I'm going to have to let you go." They said, "Fine," and they quit.

The manager was freaking out but here's what happened. Within sixty days, the sales they lost by those guys quitting and taking many of their clients with them, were eclipsed by the rest of the remaining team. The company was on a trajectory to exceed their previous sales levels with the remaining eight team members. They didn't even need to hire people to replace the ones who left.

I asked him why he thought his sales had been so good. He said, "People came to me and said, 'Thank God you finally did something with those two guys. We've been waiting for years. They always get the special exception.'" It was a clear example of criminal exchange or maybe hopeful exchange trying to get those two to emulate others' behavior. "When I finally called them out and drew the line, everybody was inspired." In this case, because the leader was serious about the rules, everyone's game lifted as a result. That's the power of a Code of Honor.

A Code of Honor is important because it adds the structure and discipline that allows your team to embody and behave in a manner consistent with the core values you have defined. In the absence of rules, people make up their own. Always! And in the heat of the battle, when emotion can run high, intelligence can run low, people resort to their instinctive behaviors, which can blow up a team, project, and even create danger.

Developing a Code of Honor creates accountability and a feeling of support. Like your values, it is a powerful statement of who you are and what your team stands for. To be effective, the code must be easy to understand and must be non-negotiable. To step out onto the playing field, you must know and agree to one set of rules.

Creating Your Code

One of the keys to your code will be deciding at what level you want to play. Lemonade Stand on the corner, or a hot, winning enterprise? A group of folks dabbling in a mutual interest or a championship team? Your code will determine your level of play, and it will also be what brings new people to your team. The stronger the code, the greater its attractive power. The clearer you are, the more like-minded people will be drawn to it.

Here are a few additional tips to drafting your Code of Honor.

1. Find sane moments in which to create the code.
When you set out to create the Code of Honor you and your team will adhere to, it is important you create it in moments of sanity. What I mean by sanity, is that you want to design your rules when you aren't under a lot of stress or frustration. You don't want your rules to be the result of knee-jerk reactions to any particular situation. Instead, they should be a valid set of protocols to tell people how to react when the heat is on.

Notice I said sane *moments*. Don't expect to come up with the perfect Code of Honor all in one sitting. It could take days, weeks, or even months. A lot of thought and consideration should go into developing the rules. You want people to be thinking clearly for this process, so you don't want to burn them out with marathon sessions. If possible, have the sessions away from the office to eliminate distractions and keep the focus on the task at hand.

2. Find recurring issues that repeatedly interfere with the performance of the team.
These are the perfect situations for determining what rules are really needed. Here's an example from *Team Code of Honor.*

I was asked by a global investment bank to work with a group of floor traders who were intelligent, adept, and fast-moving, but also arrogant and cocky. They operated like a band of roving gunslingers, and it was my job to help them become a championship team.

One of the rules they came up with in their Code of Honor said, "Public humiliation is not allowed on the trading floor." This was an important rule for governing their behavior because, in the chaotic, high-pressure environment of the trading floor, emotions and tempers can run high. This resulted in the traders, for the tiniest of reasons, yelling, screaming, and taking the heads off the back-office folks who had come onto the floor to help execute the trades. This caused huge disruptions in productivity as well as hurt feelings on the part of the back office, which sometimes led to 'getting even' scenarios.

With the rules in place, the traders policed themselves to uphold the standard. Guess what? Productivity and seamless operation between front and back office improved immediately and dramatically.

When a code is done properly, the team polices itself. This is not about the leader constantly watching the team to make sure they play by the rules. If a leader has to do that, then they really are not a team. They're just a bunch of people working for somebody else and having a paycheck being waved in their face as an incentive or disincentive. A true Code of Honor is policed by all members of the team. If you're playing football, basketball, or any other kind of competitive sport and you're not pulling your weight or you're not playing by the rules, you don't have to wait for the coach to get on your case. Your teammates will let you know pretty quickly and that's the most powerful feedback of all.

Your code needs to address your particular needs, your team's mission, and your recurring issues. The key word is recurring. If your Code of Honor tries to encompass every one-off situation, it will become unwieldy, difficult to understand, and, ultimately, ineffective. Make sure you delve beyond the surface symptoms of these issues to the real, underlying problems.

3. Everyone participates.

If you are just starting your company, you may create your code yourself, or work with your partners or core players to create the code.

If you are creating a code for an existing team, it is critical to get everyone involved. First, if the team creates it, they own it. Issuing a code from the top down and expecting everyone to buy into it is unrealistic. People need to feel ownership, which requires everyone's involvement.

Of course, if you have a large team dispersed in multiple locations, getting everyone involved in creating the code can be a bit of a trick. Our trainers have been able to help organizations facilitate this by using large

Zoom calls or conference calls. We've also broken the organization into groups and had each group submit four or five rules to the whole. Those are circulated and people vote on the ones that should stick. With some thought, you can come up with ingenious ways to involve a geographically dispersed organization in the setting of the code.

Second, it allows those who do not like the new rules to opt-out in the process. And by opt-out, I mean leave the company. They know up front what will be expected of them going forward, and either choose to play by the rules or not.

Having everyone participate in setting the rules means there will be disagreement. Well facilitated disagreements can be the catalysts that create a Code of Honor that works. The hard questions need to be asked to clarify the rules.

As the facilitator and leader of the team, it is your job to make sure everyone participates and is heard. Watch for anyone who seems to be holding back or for those team members who tend to monopolize the discussion. The first needs to be encouraged to speak and must be drawn out, the latter needs to be reined in to allow others to voice their opinions.

In some cases, it's really up to the key decision-makers or the stakeholders to be the representatives for the organization and create the code. If you're an entrepreneur with a small team, you can sit down with them and make this happen. If you're in the process of growing, you'd want to do this with team members who have been there for a while rather than with new hires. You want input from team members you trust with the mission and with your business.

On Kilimanjaro, the process for creating the Code of Honor was different. Before Kevin and Kristen ever took anyone up the mountain, the two of them sat down and came up with the non-negotiable rules each climber would be asked to abide by. Once the code is in place, it will change very little.

Think about the Ten Commandments. They were created over 2000 years ago and have not changed at all. These ten laws have become the bedrock of religions, legal systems, and moral codes. Or the United States Marine Corp, they don't change their Code of Honor. When a country or a government wants to change its Constitution to "keep up with the changing times" it becomes dangerous because they are messing with the fundamentals of the culture. The code or the rules can be further clarified. They can be more fully defined. But the original rules remain the bedrock. Once the rules are in place, you enforce them.

4. Talk about various instances of behavior and how everyone felt about them, good or bad.

I am constantly surprised when working with teams to find that people can work together for ten or fifteen years and still not know how their teammates feel about certain issues. Use the Code of Honor discussions to talk about times these issues were abused or acknowledged. The problem with unsaid stuff is that it gets acted out later in the form of rude comments, bad attitudes, or omitted details. Whenever there is resentment, sooner or later revenge rears its ugly head. This is why you must talk about the pros and cons of every issue and get to the root of people's feelings before agreeing on any rule.

5. Write it down!

As soon as you are able to decide on a rule, write it down. Post the rules in a viewable place where everyone on the team can see them. You don't want the rules to be out of sight, out of mind when a crisis or a stressful situation occurs. The rules should be stated clearly enough that anyone could explain them, even if they had no hand in setting the rules.

6. Be specific!

Your rules must be written as statements that can be acted on. Avoid any vague rules or one-word lists. It may take some doing to get the wording right; a lot of back and forth on phrasing. But it's important. Clarify, clarify, clarify.

7. Don't try to legislate moods.

Creating a rule that says, "Always be in a good mood" or "Never get angry" is not only unfair; it's unrealistic. Everyone has bad days. What you can do is say, "Don't take out your bad mood on other people."

8. Make sure the rules are somewhat of a stretch.

By this I mean your code challenges everyone on the team to be better. This will create an environment in which everyone gives their best and the team performs at a championship level.

9. Don't make too many rules.

The more rules your team needs, the more screwed up your team is. Try to shoot for a dozen or fewer rules. Any more than that and the team may begin to feel they are being micro-managed. Remember, we are addressing the recurring good and bad issues as the basis for our Code of Honor, not the one-off situations.

Enforcing the Code of Honor

Enforcing rules is not always a pleasurable task. Having to ask someone to leave the team, firing them, or removing them somehow can be awkward and hurtful. Yet, without teeth in your values, others will misinterpret, change, modify, or even use your own values against you!

To be a great Summit Leader however, is to be able to instill the Code of Honor at such a level that the team enforces the rules themselves without you having to be the traffic cop, the king, the father figure, etc. How do you do this? Simple—one of the rules is if anyone breaches a rule, anyone else on the team can 'call it.' I'll go into this in more detail in the chapter on execution, but for now, it means anyone can take the team member aside and say, "You broke the code." When done correctly, it is what distinguishes a good team from a great team. The team has to police itself. If a rule is broken and no one calls attention to it, no one takes the code, or the team, seriously.

It is human nature to test the code. Someone, yes, even you, will breach it sooner or later, maybe more than once. This is normal. The breaking of the rule is not as important as how it gets handled.

Over the years, I've been blessed to work with some amazing organizations, one of which is among the largest haircare products and most powerful beauty brands in the world. We worked hard with many of their senior teams creating Codes of Honor. I remember getting a phone call from a female director of one of the teams who said, "We have a big problem. After we went through all this effort to create these rules and this code, a very senior member of the team broke one of the rules pretty blatantly. What should I do?"

I replied with the same answer I had given the South African fellow, "Well, if you're going to create the code, you're going to have to live by it, and you may not be popular. They may call you a bitch or even other things. But if nobody else on the team is going to call it, then you're going to need to do something. Because what happens if you don't? The code and the rules will be eroded and people won't believe in it. Okay? So you know your assignment. Call me next week and tell me what happened."

I got a call back the following week. When I asked how it went, she said, "I've never been so nervous in my life. But I did it. I was pretty amazed. The person I called out knew he had done it and felt very bad about it. We were almost in tears during the conversation. He committed to never doing it again, and decided to publicly acknowledge his breach."

True to his word, he exposed himself to the group by saying, "This is what I did. I apologize. It was a complete breach of the code and it won't happen again." This level of acknowledgment and confrontation is what will allow the Code of Honor to stay in place.

As a leader, the Code of Honor must be set in a context that is far elevated from policy statements, even higher than Codes of Ethics. It is almost sacred. Those who buy into it are committed at a very deep level.

The Code of Honor is seen as something bigger than all of us. Like the Ten Commandments. If you know the story, those Ten Commandments were given by God to Moses to keep the Israelites together as a tribe amidst all the many warring, groups of the region.

It is who we want to BE, to live up to. Below I've listed my company's Code of Honor which is probably the single most powerful tool to attract those hundreds of teachers, leaders, and coaches who are part of our global organization. It's a bit more than the recommended twelve, yet it encompasses professionals in over 40 countries around the world.

BLAIR SINGER TRAINING ACADEMY
CODE OF HONOR

1. Support Blair Singer Training Academy by prioritizing:
   a. Mission first; (includes family, self, and spirit)
   b. Team second; and
   c. Individual third.
2. Never abandon a teammate in need.
3. Everyone must sell.
4. Ask more of others than they will ask of themselves.
5. Be a walking demonstration of what you teach and coach; physically, emotionally, financially, and professionally.
6. Be on time.
7. Respond to all requests within 48 business hours.
8. Take ownership and responsibility. No laying blame, justification, finger-pointing, or denial.
9. Always take action to give the highest advantage to the greatest number of people and entities with the least disadvantage to all.
10. Do whatever it takes legally, ethically, and morally to win, and celebrate all wins.
11. Deal direct, be willing to "Call it" and be "called."
12. Honor all agreements.
    a. Clear up any potential broken agreement at the first opportunity.
    b. Clean up any actual broken agreement immediately.
13. Communicate any issue to the appropriate person who is able to do something about it. Go direct!
14. Finish what you start!

15. Stay in exchange in all personal and business transactions.
16. Be honest in all transactions and communications.
17. Never abandon your post.
18. Actively engage in receiving personal development coaching on a regular basis, immerse in all BSTA materials and study sessions, and re-attend programs.
19. Full disclosure of business transactions and development.

Personal Code

One of the most important values for any team, in any family, or in any business is that of being *responsible* and *accountable*. Without them, no other rules would be enforceable. That is why the most critical rule is that each person on the team, beginning with you, agrees to take personal responsibility for their actions and for the actions of the team. We define the rule of being responsible as, "No denial, no blaming, no justifying, or excuse-making...being responsible."

That rule alone, not only has transformed my life but the lives of thousands of individuals and businesses around the world who dare to live up to it. Are we perfect? Heck no! But we care enough about ourselves to not let ourselves down.

Part of my personal Code of Honor is that I will surround myself with people who ask more of me than I ask of myself. This is really, really important. Since you're reading this book, I am going to tell you there is greatness in you. In all the hundreds of thousands of people I've worked with around the world, I have never been disappointed to find that with most there is greatness and ambition inside them. It may be buried. They may not know how to get to it, but it is there. So, one of the things I've always done to be at *my* best is to surround myself with people who are going to ask more of me than I ask of myself because I only know what I know.

Who are you surrounding yourself with? Are they stopping your greatness? Now, I'm not saying you shouldn't love them. I'm not saying to abandon them. What I am saying is that you have to demand more of them so they will demand more of you. I find many people are great but their greatness is stifled or masked or expelled by the people around them who keep them small, who keep them tapped out. If you're going to be a great Summit Leader, your job is to create the best in others and to get them to also create the best in those who surround them. You can't do it yourself. Those days are over. The 'John Wayne' days of leadership are long gone.

You need to decide what is important to you and those around you. Your personal code is a testimony to who you are and it sends a message to your team. What problems or patterns have you created for yourself in the past you'd like to resolve and finally take control of once and for all? What will you truly adhere to and hold yourself accountable for? Long after you're gone, people will remember more about what you stood for than what you earned.

Keep in mind, your personal Code of Honor must be in sync with the company's Code of Honor. If they are too far out of alignment, you may be able to tolerate the disconnects for a period, but eventually they'll cause frustration and resentment. Your personal Code of Honor insists that you call yourself out as well when you know you've broken a rule.

Everyone on the team has the right and the responsibility to 'call out' breaches of the code to the person who breaches it. To do this requires, what Google defined in their 2012 'Project Aristotle' study of teams, 'psychological safety.' You must create an environment that allows members to feel safe from attack, retribution, and emotional or psychological warfare. We'll talk more about how to do this in the chapter on execution.

The participative process of identifying values and explaining and agreeing to the Code of Honor rules helps to foster a safe environment. It is the single most powerful tool for building, recruiting, and empowering teams. It has been the pivot point for countless case studies of the businesses we have worked with around the world in nearly every industry over the last three decades.

Chapter Seven

Protocols

*"Do not pray for an easy life,
pray for the strength to endure a difficult one."*
—*Bruce Lee*

So far, we've gone through a lot of different steps. But how does it all lay out? How do you put it all to use in your business?

We start with a mission, something that's bigger than all of us. Something that motivates and inspires. Something we may never actually complete but for which we are striving.

Next, we have to identify our reasons why. Everyone on the team has to have a reason why that they identify with personally.

The third step is to identify the values we all hold important to us. Because in times of strife and discrepancy and upset, we're going to want to fall back on those values. Remember, when emotion is high, intelligence is low. Values provide the framework for how we will behave.

Based on our values we create rules, a Code of Honor, a way we operate in good times and in bad times. From these rules come protocols. Protocols are the processes, systems, and set of rules formed to protect some core value that is paramount in your business, family, or group. They are the official set of procedures for what action to take in a certain situation. Protocols provide specifics and examples around the expected behaviors for embodying a company's core values. In this way, there is no room for misinterpretation by any team member.

So, for example, if 'never abandon a teammate in need' is one of the rules based on the values of your organization, what does the protocol for that rule look like? Well, if someone is working late and they're falling behind, the protocol would be to ask, "What can we do to help?" This doesn't mean we're necessarily going to do their work for them, but what could we do to support them? Maybe one person stays behind to help. Maybe we split the work into shifts.

Here's another example of the protocol of 'no team member left behind' from the book *Endurance: Shackleton's Incredible Voyage* by Alfred Lansing. It's the story of Ernest Shackleton taking his team to Antarctica and becoming stranded for ten months when their ship was trapped by pack ice. The ship was eventually crushed and his crew spent another five months surviving on ice floes until they too disintegrated. He got his crew on lifeboats and sailed across rough seas to reach Elephant Island. There, the crew spent another four months while Shackleton sailed off for help. It took four rescue missions to get all of his men to safety.

On a ship, people stand watch. No matter how exhausted they were, no matter how frozen and frostbitten they were, there would be four people on watch for four hours. When they were in the small 22-foot boats, they were bailing and sailing as the others slept. This shifting of the watch is part of what kept Shackleton's crew alive and thriving. Had they not had these protocols, they may not have survived. Their protocol was set on a strict set of rules forged from their value of 'we will get through this together.' We, as a team, will survive, no matter what the odds are, and against 40 and 60-foot seas, icebergs, freezing rain, cold, and lack of nutrition.

They stuck together and got everybody through. But the only way that happened is because they followed strict protocols that were based on core values. They had a mission. The first mission was to get to the South Pole. That failed. The next mission was to get home alive. Everybody. What were their values? Take care of everyone. These rules under extreme conditions created the protocols that literally kept them alive.

Protocol on Kilimanjaro

Our guides, Kevin and Kristin, also embody the value of 'no team member left behind' and have rules and protocols in place to support this value. If you recall, Kevin broke his back in high school while playing basketball. He went off to college but had a horrible freshman year. Without the sports he was so used to playing, he just didn't know what to do. Then a friend invited him to go to Oregon to have some fun and climb Mount Hood. It was an experience that would change the trajectory of his life; one that would then help thousands of people and save countless lives.

It was the first time he had ever climbed a mountain. And it was the first time in his life he'd ever experienced a true team sport, where life and death might hang in the air. Climbing is a team sport. One thing every person who climbs Kilimanjaro will say is that they wouldn't have made it without the team. Now that's not just a nicety or a platitude. It's a reality. When one person is down, someone else is up, and everybody helps each other through each day.

For the most part, climbing Kili is safe and few people face death, but it can happen. With that sense of life and death urgency, rules and protocols become critically important and have a direct repercussion if they are not followed.

As I mentioned earlier, on Kilimanjaro Kevin and Kristen make the rules. Not me. Not any of the rest of us. That agreement is fundamental. With safety and health as the underlying core values, each rule is not only explained but intensely enforced if broken.

Rules like: Sanitizing or washing hands before and after every pee break, and before entering the dining tent; Never passing the lead guide on the trail; Leaving camp at 9:00 am sharp; Not coming to the meal tent until you are packed; Drinking 3+ liters of water a day; Eating enough; Disclosing how your body is feeling if anything comes up physically; Telling the truth about your medical condition and all medications; Not ingesting any medication without clearing it with Kristen first.

We have porters who carry all of our gear. These are amazing human beings with unbelievable strength, grace, and kindness. Respect is a core value of our climb: for the mountain, for them, and for each other. Therefore, the rule is we cannot put more than forty pounds into the gear bag they carry for each of us. It would jeopardize their health and safety.

On the mountain, there is a set of protocols for abiding by the rules. There is a daily schedule of waking, packing, eating, saddling up, stepping, breathing, following, resting, and sleeping. Some of the protocols may seem a bit annoying or non-essential, but the guides insist. Why? Because when asked out of the blue what the number one value or priority is for them on the mountain, there is no hesitation...SAFETY. From that view, it all makes sense. Example: Stop moving if you want to take pictures. Otherwise, you could trip or fall, and not only end your climb but put the rest of the team at risk.

Some had a really difficult time following those protocols. Some climbers struggled as a result. Others did not struggle but held up the team in the process. For example...no talking in your tent before 6:30 am. Why? So others in the campsite can sleep and gain every minute of precious rest they will need for the climb.

At our nightly debriefs, we would discuss these protocols as a team and how they applied to the core values of K2. It was clear that the protocols were critical to protecting each of us. On Kili, the protocols tightly reflect the rules. They are very decisive in the moment. In other words, no, you will not take that medicine and yes, you will drink four liters of water.

REMEMBER THIS, (if nothing else): THE CODE OF HONOR AND THE PROTOCOLS THAT COME FROM IT ARE DESIGNED TO **PROTECT YOU FROM YOU!!!**

The Importance of Protocols to You

When we identified the core values of businesses, we looked at what protocols we had put in place over the years and how well they reflected the rules. What we discovered was that in business our protocols were much looser. Some of this has to do with it being life or death on the mountain and it rarely being that dire in our businesses. Still, without tight protocols, chaos and mediocre results can occur.

I know for myself, I was not always definitive enough in my business. I'd say, well, let's try it and see how it goes, or these are the guidelines we want to follow right now, we'll discuss them again next week. I wasn't decisive in the moment. That was a big "AHA" for me. Quick and decisive decision-making as opposed to just kind of laying it out there hoping for the best and not trying to ruffle too many feathers.

One of the protocols we identified we could all get better at was to create and identify narrow time boundaries. Kevin and Kristen were always very clear to tell us to never ask about what was going to happen tomorrow or the next day. We were only allowed to ask about today. It was one step at a time, one camp at a time. We were told about how many hours we would be climbing and what to expect, but nothing more. Everything was compartmentalized into understandable and limited time frames. Wake up to breakfast, hiking to lunch, hiking to camp, unpacking and rest, afternoon tea, debrief, and dinner, then sleep.

This was another big learning for me. My natural tendency is to be all over the board, with dozens of overlapping projects priorities and obligations. My organization was typically not one step at a time. We'd follow step after step until something else jumped up and grabbed our attention and then we'd be off working on the new shiny thing.

One of the reasons people face overwhelm is because they're distracted by so many shiny objects. They don't have a definitive plan. A product we use to assist entrepreneurs to avoid the shiny object lure is called PERT: Project Evaluation Review Technique. I'll talk more about this later. But the process is designed to focus all the efforts toward one particular goal. That doesn't mean you can't have multiple goals. You might have five different goals but you'll also have five different plans for each of those goals. The key, and what PERT helps you do, is ensuring the five plans interact with each other in a way that is productive and effective for the business.

Another reason people face overwhelm is that they don't have a team or they have the wrong team. Again, I'll touch more on this later.

I've put the one-step protocol into practice in my personal life as well. I have a daily routine. The first thing I do when I get up is drink 16 ounces of water. I brush my teeth. I make my bed. Then I start my "Miracle Morning" (Hal Alrod) routine, which includes some meditation, affirmations, visualizations, exercise, reading, and journaling. It may take me an hour to get into my day, but my day works because I have this directed routine. It allows my mind to be at rest because I know exactly the steps I'm going to follow.

I always say that most people cannot plan past lunch. Long-term goals and strategies are fine and even necessary, but to keep a team focused you have to shrink the space. You can't get too far ahead of yourself. In business, when you are doing new things, you don't really want to do them off the seat of your pants. You need to think in terms of process. Decide upfront that we're going to work this plan step by step. Sure, unexpected things will happen that will mess with the plan. But having the initial focus and presence around the process makes your job as a leader responding to surprises that much easier. In all these years since that first summit, I've learned there's a lot of emotional and mental release and comfort in knowing and understanding Kilimanjaro's number one important lesson, that it's simply **One Step at a Time**.

Just as with core values, you want to take an appropriate amount of time to understand exactly what protocols best support your values and how to effectively implement them. Protocols will assist in recruiting, inspiring, and aligning your teams, however, too many can be seen as micromanaging and quelching creativity.

Chapter Eight

Recruiting Your Team

"Find the right people, not the best people."

—Jack Ma

"How many of you here, would like to go to Kilimanjaro?" This is a question I ask audiences around the world after I have shared a little of my experience there, and after showing a simple three-minute video. Typically, about a third of the group will raise their hands. Two-thirds do not. For one-third, it seems inspiring, adventurous, and a 'good idea.'

For others, it's nice, but not their cup of tea. That's good! Because the big lesson of recruiting is that whatever you are recruiting for, will not be for everyone. Of the one-third whom we invite to an information call, half show up. Of that group, another two-thirds realize that it's going to take some work and they bow out. We are left with those who are truly pulled by the mountain to explore it.

For those folks, their journey up the mountain has already begun. The mental, emotional, and physical climb to become a person who CAN summit Kili begins right away.

The people you surround yourself with will determine your success in life. And your wealth. What I have learned in business is that money and promises of acknowledgment are poor attractors if you are looking to build a great team. As mentioned earlier, your mission, your core values, and your Code of Honor are your primary recruiting tools. These three intrinsic concepts should allow each potential candidate to answer the question, "Why would I come to work with your organization?" And, for existing team members, "Why should I continue to work with you?" Notice I used the words work *with you*, not *for you*. The best team members are not interested in a master/slave relationship, but one of collaboration, innovation, and personal growth. Those leaders who can offer something compelling will attract the right team.

Candidates today are interviewing you as much as you are interviewing them. Let's say you're at a job fair and you've got several candidates lined up to see you. They're all qualified and any of them might be able to be a part of your dream team. How do you choose among them? Here's something I regularly do. I start by telling them our mission is to create the best teachers, leaders, and facilitators in the world to change the way we learn and help entrepreneurs succeed. Then I ask, "Why do you want to work with us?" The first candidate says, "Well, I really like your company, and, you know, it seems like a good opportunity. The pay and the benefits are good." The second candidate responds with, "I'm really turned on by the mission. I think if I can be a part of this organization, I'm going to grow. Your benefits are great, but I'm more intrigued by the mission and how I would be able to impact other people."

Obviously, I'm going to hire the second candidate because I can see their values are in line with the values and the mission of my organization. I believe a person should be a part of the team for the reasons of the mission, as opposed to just for the money. In my mode of leadership, that is what is important. If I look at my entire entrepreneurial career, it has been team members who were mission-driven more than money-driven, who have bailed me out of just about every problem. In one company, I had team members saying, "We'll work for free. If we have to defer our income for a little while we'll do it. We don't want to let this thing go."

It's this kind of commitment to mission that really has kept me and my businesses alive and allowed us to thrive. So, rather than hoping this is the response you'll get, start with a person whose mind is already there because of the mission. You've got to compensate people properly. But money becomes secondary when they're there for the mission. They're there because they want to be. Whatever it is you're trying to do as an organization, they want to get that done. It isn't all altruistic either. On the self-serving side, they want to become a better person themselves and they see your organization as a way to get there.

A great team is not just a group of people with a common objective. It is a group committed to working together toward a common goal in which each person's unique abilities will be tested and stretched to the fullest. A great team welcomes the challenge, even though sometimes it can be messy, frustrating, and not at all fun. They value the results they will achieve both personally and for the company.

I have never been a high-paying employer, and I have never promised things I cannot deliver. But my promise to those who come to Kili is that whatever happens, the person who comes off the mountain will be the biggest and best version of themselves they have experienced to date. Perhaps you are thinking, "Well, that's because it's Kili." Yet, this is the same promise I make in my business, the same one John F. Kennedy promised when he set the goal to go to the moon in the 1960s:

> *"We choose to go to the moon in this decade and do the other things. Not because it is easy, but because it is hard. Because that goal will serve to organize and measure the best of our energies and skills. Because that challenge is one that we are willing to accept. One we are unwilling to postpone. And one we intend to win."*

Recruitment Is a Leader's Responsibility

Too often, companies rely on software programs and corporate recruiters to find the candidates for their teams. These are fine screening devices if you use them only to get yourself to a shortlist. But at some level, if you've got to hire for some key position, you have to talk to them. You've got to make sure your conversation counts, that it makes a difference.

I've helped many organizations, large and small, with this. HR would receive a shortlist of candidates and they would be the first to talk with them. The frontline may have told HR that they need an analyst with certain criteria. I'd say, "Okay, I got all that. But what else do they need? That's the technical side. What do you need on the behavior side? Do you need somebody who's a team player? Somebody who works on their own? Somebody who's a maverick? What are you trying to create?" These are important questions to ask, and if HR isn't asking them, the leader of the team should be supplying the information.

Here's an example of how bad it can be when you aren't asking the right questions to screen candidates. I was working with a large investment bank that was having trouble with their sales teams being able to garner new business. I would sit in on their calls and then analyze the call later. It was tough having to tell senior management that their team was so busy trying to upsell the client, they weren't truly listening to the client.

An investment manager from one of their clients was on the phone. I sat in the conference room with about ten of the investment bank's people. The bankers asked the client a question or two, and then they put the phone on mute. They then started talking among themselves, coming up with a myriad of ideas and solutions for the client. The problem was that no one was listening to what the client was saying.

They then took off the mute and let him talk for a little bit longer. Oblivious to the client's concerns, the bankers responded by saying, "Yeah, we got it but, I think we have a good solution for you." You could hear the customer saying, "Well, I'm not sure. I would need to talk this over with my committee." The bankers continued their relentless pitching until the client found a way to excuse themselves from the call.

When they hung up the phone, I asked them how they thought it went. They said, "Well, I don't know. It's a perfect solution but he didn't seem so happy about it." I asked if they had any thoughts as to why. They didn't. So, I explained. "It's because you weren't even freaking listening. If you had been listening you would have heard his concern because of the last debacle with you guys. He said he was losing face in the eyes of his committee. He's got shareholders pounding on him. His boss is all over him. He mentioned these and other issues but not one of you guys heard it."

So, why is this example relevant? Well, if we backtrack to where these bankers got hired, we see they were hired because they were at the top of their class. They were the best and the brightest. These guys were rogue, maverick gunslingers. When you get them all in one room, you're not getting a team. There is little client focus and almost no empathy. Solutions matter more than people. They care about themselves and they care about their commissions.

This goes back to recruiting. Who are you recruiting and why? This is an example of what happens when you get the wrong guys in the wrong job because you didn't screen them, or you, as the owner or leader, weren't clear. You didn't think about the job from a mission and values perspective. You were just trying to fill a position with the best and the brightest. Well, you need to define what the best and the brightest means in your organization.

When recruiting those who want to become great leaders and teachers, I explain our mission and how it was developed. I also give them no guarantees other than if they join with us, they will experience the best version of themselves. And it works. People come prepared to pay a lot of money (that's right, *they* pay *us*) to be trained to be part of an elite team of educators who are changing the marketplace.

If you were to ask any of our trainers around the world why they are part of Blair Singer Training Academy, without hesitation they will respond, "Mission."

Yet, like everything else, not everyone goes the distance. Their WHY gets challenged. Mission doesn't come first with them. Their needs or desires win out. They succumb to the sirens of Ulysses.

Going after the next shiny thing is a constant challenge for most entrepreneurs. You're always looking at what other people are doing in their marketing or their business. "Wow, that looks like a really good idea. I want to do that." So, you shift part of your marketing over to what others are doing, and then you find when it doesn't work that you've got to start that process all over again. You get distracted.

With today's technology, it's so easy to get distracted: Facebook ads, a new click funnel, a different kind of lead generation system, and all that stuff are always tempting you. Often you end up getting small returns because what you don't see behind the scenes is the tremendous amount of work those who have mastered these systems have gone through.

I was on a coaching call with one of my clients who is also a coach. He was expressing how frustrated he was because he wasn't getting the results he wanted. As I listened to him talk about his plan for the coming week, I realized he was once again drifting. The week before he had been working on a different offering to his clients. A couple weeks before that, he had decided to only work with entrepreneurs to help them earn more. Before that his plan was to help people obtain financial freedom in their life. I said, "Dude, hold on a second. What are you doing? Focus on one thing and give yourself a chance to win." He was spinning his wheels and gaining no ground.

This is a classic example of why mission comes first. When you stay true to your mission, your core values, and the protocols that support them, you stay focused; you take one step at a time.

Think back to my conversation with Retired 3-Star General Jack Bergman regarding how he managed to recruit Marines. Considering the pay scale is not great, the working conditions are pretty rough, and life and death are on the line, there had to be something pretty powerful to inspire people to enlist. I remember his answer distinctly. "These young people want to be part of something bigger than themselves. They want to become Marines because of who they can BECOME."

Of course, not everyone wants to become a Marine. Just like not everyone wants to climb Kili. Just like not everyone wants to be in my business, and not everyone wants to work with you. But those leaders who can help grow people, who can offer them a part of something bigger than themselves, will attract the right people for the right reasons.

Chapter Nine

Teaching and Learning

"The mediocre teacher tells. The good teacher explains.
The superior teacher demonstrates.
The great teacher inspires."

—*William Arthur Ward*

There is a secret to leadership that I learned long ago: Leaders must be teachers. They must educate, inspire and empower... and embrace life-long learning.

Leaders Must Be Teachers

This hidden fact is the secret to organizational greatness and is nearly completely overlooked by the market. Every entrepreneur wants a team who can think, solve problems, communicate, collaborate, and take responsibility. Right? Where are they going to learn it?

In school? No way. For a very long time now, the focus in schools has been on having students pass standardized tests. Teachers don't have the time, and in my opinion, few of them have the leadership talent, to teach life skills like cooperation, collaboration, and learning to work together to solve problems. Don't get me wrong, I've had a handful of wonderful teachers who really *taught* me, but most of them were professional 'tellers.'

Even when a team project is assigned, it's usually one or two people who do all the work and end up being frustrated and angry at the others on the team. That frustration is the best training of all because that is life.

It's not the history lesson we're trying to do as a group, it's all the garbage you've got to handle with your team to be able to get a result. That's the root; the main event. It would be great if most schoolteachers understood this concept but they don't. Yes, we will get the project done. But what are you learning about people? And what are you learning about yourself?

I want to tell you a story to illustrate my point. As a Rich Dad Advisor, I volunteered to come into my son's class once a month and do a lesson on financial literacy. I think he was in the third grade. I put the class in teams and I said, "Okay, here's your job. Your job is to create a product and sell it to the public. You can't sell it to your parents. We're going to see who makes the most money."

This was a really simple project. They were all excited. The following month, I put them back into their teams and it was just total chaos in the room. I thought to myself, *Oh, this is good.* And I asked them, "Who would like to share?"

One kid said, "I made the product. I sold the product. And I collected the money. But nobody else did anything." Other kids started talking about what they did and started complaining about their team members who didn't keep their word... it was a blizzard of finger-pointing, blaming and complaining. Kids were getting angry and the teachers started to freak out feeling the class was spiraling out of control. The teachers were in a panic. They were about ready to stop me. I thought it was all perfect.

Then I said, "So, what are you all learning?"

Silence...

There was a young boy sitting on the floor, kind of by himself amid all this commotion, wearing a floppy, Rustafarian-style hat. He raised his hand. I called on him. "Yes, what is it? What'd you learn? What are you learning?"

He said, "Mr. Singer, I learned this. I think money is really easy. People are really the problem."

I cracked up. "Dude, you are going to be a rich man. Someday you're going to be a very wealthy entrepreneur."

It was a great lesson for a young third grader. How true was his conclusion? I think that's real education. But our public school system doesn't really care about that. The teachers were still freaked out at their loss of control.

I sometimes think it would be better if we went back to the way older students were taught in the mid-1800s. Kids learned from real mentors out in the workplace and really learned the lessons they needed to learn.

Today, organizations like Nissan and Toyota and others have created their own universities and their own schools to prepare kids for their workplaces. They teach engineering, team development, collaboration, communication, etc. Why? Because they have come to realize that the current public school system is not equipping the workforce of the future. They are replacing high-priced public universities with their own schools and then actually offering well-paying jobs.

In this day and age, a Summit Leader is a 'Teacher/Leader.' It is clear the school systems of the world have not taught most of us how to work in teams, how to communicate, how to master our minds, change our habits, form solid relationships, adapt to changing environments, be financially literate, etc.

So where do we learn those things? From those leaders who also understand their roles as teachers. In business alone, there are hundreds of lessons being thrown at us every day. Great leaders see their businesses as schools. And if our business is a school, it's our job to be the teachers. Not just teaching sales, training, and IT, but lessons on collaboration, communication, and life lessons on relationships, ethics, and service.

In today's rapidly changing environment, where more and more business is being done remotely, and more and more processes are automated, it becomes even more critical for leaders to teach people skills to their teams. In Jeff Booth's book, *The Price of Tomorrow,* he talks about the speed of technology doubling, tripling, and quadrupling in less and less time. That genie is not going back into the bottle, it's accelerating. Therefore, it's even more critical that you become a Summit Leader. You must understand your job is less about technical know-how and more about being able to teach your team how to behave in a way that's conducive with their job, with their environment, and with those around them. If you don't, you won't succeed, at least not for very long. Not to mention you'll attract the wrong players to your team.

As mentioned in the introduction, Po Chung, the co-founder of DHL International, addressed this at an even higher level when he said to me it was a "societal responsibility for those in business to teach their knowledge to their leaders and those who come after them."

At present, the BEST way for you to help your team grow and develop is for you, as a leader, to teach them.

In every business, your greatest asset is your team. Yet the greatest liability is that team's inability to communicate. Every day there are valuable lessons to be learned. The ultimate form of leadership is the ability to teach your team how to be successful—not by telling them, or reciting a monologue on how to do something, or by telling them what you did, but by getting them involved, practicing, drilling, challenging them, and getting them dirty in the process.

You don't learn to play ball by just watching game films. You don't learn to raise kids just by doing what your parents did. You don't build a business from a book, and you certainly don't learn how to be a great team player by being told how to do it. You have to be taught!

In my company, there is a general rule that anybody who works for me or works with us has got to consume all of the programs we teach to the public. Part of the training is you've got to **do** the training. People do it. That's primary. We also teach other business skills such as sales, marketing, planning, communicating, problem solving....and the other protocols that are a part of our business.

We also mentor and teach people skills. For example, how do you deal with a customer who may be upset about something? We ask them to tell us how they would handle it, and then we give them some feedback on that process. We help them to role-play the situation before they encounter it.

Teaching is a combination of leading, selling, motivating, and involving. Education does not mean cramming data down someone's throat. It means repetition and discovery. For example, the more you experience the act of selling, by repeating it and drilling it, the more you discover how it works, how to apply it, and how to get rich.

The thousands of entrepreneurs I have coached over the years have learned to become master facilitators. They have learned how to create an environment of learning, growing, and responsibility. Their businesses have gone on to make millions of dollars through good and difficult times. They have become great teachers and a leaders, not preachers!

Over the course of my career, I have found this is a promise I can deliver on. It's not easy. Being a teacher/leader is not for everyone. But when the bullets are flying, it's good to know you have the right people there for the right reasons.

Yes, it's going to be hard. It may be uncertain. There may be ups and downs. But at the end of the day, if you play by our Code of Honor, you will become the person you want to be.

I have worked with and coached some of the best Fortune 500 companies in the world. Those leaders who have heeded this message, have built some of the most amazing teams in their industries and moved their corporate dials in big ways.

Leaders Must Be Learners

A leader will only be an effective teacher if they are also a lifelong learner.

I'm sure you've heard the saying, 'lead by example.' Well, when it comes to developing your team, what you do is more important than what you say. If you want your team to continue learning and growing, they must see you embracing the concept. Sure, it's an investment in time and money but successful leaders who are constantly in learning mode develop stronger leadership skills than their peers.

Dr. Brad Staats, associate professor of operations at the University of North Carolina and author of the book, *Never Stop Learning: Stay Relevant, Reinvent Yourself, and Thrive* says, "Today's fast-paced, ever-changing, global economy requires us to never stop learning or we risk becoming irrelevant. Savvy leaders recognize this means investing in their own learning journey, so they can develop the processes and behaviors required for ongoing success."

Leaders who don't push themselves to continuously learn risk falling behind. They lack the ability to generate new ideas, solve problems from new perspectives, and grow complacent and stale in their jobs. Worse yet, team members become disenchanted with the organization when it isn't responding to the changes in environment, technology, and competition. Eric Hoffer, an American moral and social philosopher said, "In a time of drastic change, it is the learners who inherit the future. The learned (those who stopped learning) usually find themselves equipped to live in a world that no longer exists."

There are numerous ways for leaders to learn. You can read, listen to podcasts, engage in question-and-answer periods during presentations, go to conferences, join a master mind group, and, my personal favorite, one-on-one coaching. This list is by no means exclusive. Learning happens everywhere when you are in learning mode. Some of the best learning opportunities are when you are teaching and discovering what your team has learned.

Learning even comes from outside your job responsibilities: take a cooking class, learn to play a musical instrument, volunteer at a nonprofit or study a new language. These new activities stimulate your brain and expand your creativity and critical thinking. Learning something totally outside of your normal wheelhouse opens your mind to attack problems from a different viewpoint. It can burn new neurological pathways in your brain and thus challenge your old assumptions and bring new tools to the table.

Climbing Kilimanjaro was a massive out-of-the-box lesson I learned without even realizing it. At least not on the first climb. But coming down from the summit on the second climb, it hit me like a ton of bricks. I had learned so much about myself. And not just myself, I learned how what Kristen and Kevin had done leading us up that mountain could be applied to leaders everywhere. I kept going back, and I'll keep going back for the same reason. Each time I go, I learn something new. Sometimes it's from the mountain, sometimes it's from one of my fellow hikers, but most often, it's a spiritual kind of learning on the inside. Since I'm totally unplugged from the outside world, I have time to get a good perspective on my business and on my life. It's a big win for me and a big learning— particularly discovering nuances to things I thought I had already learned.

You've probably realized by now I am a huge proponent of personal development. In my organization, I insist that every team member do personal development training outside of our company. That may seem pretty radical, but I've had personal development coaching for myself, for the last 25-30 years. So, I tell people, if you're going to work for me you've got to do it too.

No matter your level of mastery, there is always more to learn.

Chapter Ten

Preparation and Training

"Being nervous isn't bad.
It just means something important is happening."
—Michael Jordan

There are two parts of any journey, project, or mission. The task itself, obviously. But the most critical part of the journey is the preparation and training for the task. It is popular to say that 80 percent of life is just showing up. I clearly disagree. If you just "show up" to Kilimanjaro without spending hours, days, months, and miles preparing, you will get spanked.

The key is to learn to love all the parts: the preparation, the training, and the journey. To love the burn in your quadriceps, the sweat dripping off your nose in the gym, as well as the hours of solitude walking or hiking in the lead-up to Kilimanjaro. Lots of people want to go to the summit, but few are willing to put in the work.

You have to learn to love both parts. Why? What if you turn your ankle or you can't cope with the altitude and you have to turn back? Is the whole thing a loss? Not if you were loving and learning from both parts.

Preparation

Lots of mental stress comes from not knowing how to prepare for the unknown. Preparation is a key factor in reducing fear, anxiety, and the losses that come from unexpected disasters. For some, planning comes naturally, while others prefer to deal with problems and situations as they occur. I get the idea of planning and preparation can seem boring, particularly if you're an adrenaline junkie like me who loves the buzz of activity. The advantage to being prepared, however, is that you can more quickly and efficiently manage what life throws at you because, to some extent, you already have the solutions at hand.

Before we ever set foot on Kilimanjaro, we underwent a lot of preparation. For months, weeks, and even the day before the climb, Kevin and Kristen were preparing us, because none of us knew anything about climbing a mountain. We were all a bunch of middle-aged flatlanders.

We had regular team meetings by video. They taught us to breathe properly, how to step properly, what to take and not take in our backpacks, how to pack properly, and more. We were shown how to pack our day packs, so they didn't overweight us, but we had access to things we would need during the day. Kevin pulled out his whole backpack and laid it all out on the ground, showing us what he had and the order he was putting it in, and why. We learned how to dress on different days and what shoes to wear.

For those of us who lived in, or near, Arizona they conducted training hikes. We'd go to Mount Humphreys in Flagstaff because it's at 12,000 feet and would give us some experience climbing in altitude. Then they would take a crew to the Grand Canyon to climb. They set goals for us regarding how many miles we should hike each week with instructions on how we should do the hikes. Then they'd follow up, asking what we had accomplished.

They did everything they possibly could in advance to make sure we were prepared. We learned to be comfortable with our gear, our bodies, and our tasks. It eliminated a whole chunk of potential anxiety about what might happen on the mountain.

I once had the opportunity to attend a talk given by Mayor Giuliani, who happened to be the mayor of New York City at the time of the 9/11 terrorist attack. He said that one of the reasons they had relative success in dealing with the 9/11 disaster is that for weeks, months, even years prior, the city organizations practiced every single possible emergency and contingency they could think of.

They practiced potential earthquakes, potential fires, potential floods, hijackings, every kind of disaster. Giuliani said, "The one thing we did not plan on happening was planes flying into buildings. But because we had practiced everything else, all the city agencies, fire department, police department, social workers, hospitals, and health care workers all snapped right into play, even though they had not prepared for that event."

I feel that today, with what the world is throwing at all of us, we, my team, my friends, the Rich Dad Advisors, we've been practicing for this our entire lives. This is what we spent the 1980s, 1990s, and the early 2000s practicing: working on our little voices, working on how to learn, how to challenge ourselves, how to keep trying new things. And now, when all the craziness hits the fan, we're prepared. I feel pity for the people right now who have been living the cushioned life and have not stepped out of the box to learn how to think and prepare themselves for any contingency.

With technology evolving as fast as it is, many jobs we take for granted today will be gone; not in a matter of years, but in a matter of months. Those people who have been training, not for a new job necessarily, but training on how to make changes, on how to remain cool in the eye of the storm, will do well. Those who don't will panic and will fall prey to somebody else's plan and somebody else's point of view, which may or may not be good. As a leader, you can't afford that. You've got to always be prepared for what comes next.

How many times have you thrown your team into a task and let them just figure it out? Whether the team was successful or not, it most likely took them longer to achieve and caused all kinds of anxiety and stress.

The difference between being proactive and being reactive is being prepared. I'm not saying you can't or shouldn't be flexible or that you have to rigidly control everything. But one of the benefits of being prepared is that it can actually enhance your flexibility. By spending some time upfront with various "what if" scenarios, when something unexpected does occur, you can respond quicker and more effectively. Analyzing those what-ifs also strengthens your ability for strategic thinking. That's what Kevin and Kristen employed before they ever took anyone up the mountain. For them, strategic thinking, analyzing all the what-ifs, and having a plan in place to deal with them meant the difference between everyone getting up and down the mountain safely or not.

For those of us in business, thinking strategically and being prepared is what gives us a competitive edge. It provides resilience; the capacity to recover quickly when something bad happens. When you've prepared, you aren't second-guessing when something unexpected shows up. There's no guilt or bitter taste in your mouth as a result of knowing you could have done more.

One of the simplest methods for preparing for any mission or project is to start with the end in mind and work backwards from there. It is the quintessential step-by-step process of how to get something done. You start in the future with what you want, then work your way back to the present, creating all of the milestone events that will need to take place for you to get what you want to happen. Basically, you create what we referred to earlier as a PERT chart: Program Evaluation Review Technique.

In 1957, the Special Projects Office of the United States Navy developed the PERT chart to guide the Polaris Nuclear Submarine Missile project. It is still widely used today. It's a visual, freeform representation used to map out and track the tasks and timelines for getting a project done. The major milestones of the project are represented by either boxes or circles with directional or diversional arrows denoting the critical path of the tasks to meet those milestones.

That's about as technical as I'm going to get explaining PERT charts. Our trainers are trained on how to help high-performance entrepreneurs or leaders create high-performance plans, and how to architect and design their future, rather than being a victim to it. There are numerous articles and videos on our YouTube channel and on our website to explain the process. The reason I feel PERT charts are so effective is they do what I said in Chapter 6 was so important: They help you to focus, to narrow the space, to take one step at a time.

Do you remember the guy I talked about who was jumping from one shiny object to another almost every week and wondering why nothing was sticking?

I told him, "Let's go back to the beginning. You've basically got no business. You are invisible. In business when you are invisible, the formula is to 'serve first.'" I told him to go out and get a couple of friends, people he'd coached in the past, and tell them he's going to coach them for free for the next three months. The idea was to get some case studies from those people, then analyze what they say he did very well, then build a business from there. And forget about all those other things.

He'd gone overboard. We re-grounded him. Now his business is flourishing. I can speak to this freely because I've done this many times myself. I jump all over the place, too. One of the reasons I go back to Kili every year is to get myself centered; to remind myself to eliminate the unnecessary and let go. When you get above the cloud line on Kili, the things below don't seem nearly as important as they did when you were in front of them. Going back to the beginning of your business is a way of pushing all the 'stuff' aside and getting to the priorities of what is important to you. Focus. One step at a time. Breathe. One step at a time. Breathe.

Training

Preparation alone is not enough. It doesn't matter how great a plan you have if no one on your team knows how to execute it. Consider this riddle very few people get the answer to:

Three frogs were sitting on a log. One of the frogs decided to jump into the pond. How many frogs are left on the log?

If you answered 2, you're wrong. Three frogs are still sitting on the log. Just because one frog decided to jump, doesn't mean he did. Deciding isn't acting. It's only when you put decision together with action that you get results. Preparing is the deciding phase. Training begets action.

For training to work, it must be incremental in difficulty, consist of a disciplined routine of repetition, employ a measurable level of accountability, and be mentored from a consistently reliable source.

Technical Training

Training consists of two parts. The first is the technical development skills necessary to perform the tasks at hand.

For example, if you are training a team to sell, you would start by first teaching the basics of communication and meeting people. You would NOT show them a 10-minute video and send them out into the market. You would have them spend twenty to thirty minutes per week perfecting their introductions and role-playing objections as you incrementally introduce them to the entire selling cycle. The number of calls, contacts, and appointments they make would be reported daily, and someone who has become proficient in the process would mentor and coach them to proficiency.

Nobody learns how to play golf by just teeing up the ball and expecting it all to work. There are different parts to learning the game of golf: there's driving the ball; there's the middle game; there's the short game; there's the game out of the trap; there's the putting game. In order to master any process, you must first master each element of the process. I'll say it again. In order to master anything you want to learn to do, you have to master the individual pieces of it. One of my mentors said, "That's how every master becomes a master; by understanding the integrity of becoming a master of anything is mastering the parts of the whole." You can't try to master the whole all at once because that's just not going to happen.

Learning to sell is the same thing. So, we lay out the selling cycle. We teach a sales team how to map out the steps of the selling cycle. Maybe the first step is a cold call. The second step is an appointment. The third step might be a demonstration. Master each step. Get proficient at each one. Get trained in each one until you are really good. Then move on to the next one. Then the next one, and then the next one. It may take a little bit longer but you're going to have a lot of team members who are really good at sales if you do it this way.

Then, when you're starting to calibrate what they're doing, you take the map of the selling process and you measure each piece. How many cold calls did you do? How many appointments did you have? How many demonstrations did you do? How many proposals. This allows you to quickly see where a person is deficient and they can see for themselves what they need to work on. This is training. It's measured by the numbers.

I encourage leaders to take almost every process they train people in and organize it into a cycle, particularly sales. Sales are the lifeblood of your business. Get people accustomed to being accountable to the process. Then they will have the ability to improve and improve quickly.

Debrief as a Training Tool

Once we reach each of our camps, everyone unpacks into their tents, changes clothes, and we meet inside a big geodesic dome tent. Sitting in folding chairs, supplied with hot tea, coffee, cocoa, and popcorn, we debrief the day. It becomes my job as a leader to facilitate the lifelong learning of the day by pulling lessons from the group. There are huge "AHAs," sometimes tears, and lots of laughter. Each person's experience is different and therefore their lessons are unique. But somehow the lesson for one is the lesson for all.

Let me give you an example of a dear friend who is an amazing, world-class interior designer from Malaysia who went up to Kilimanjaro with us. His name is Su Chang. He struggled a lot. He was under the weather half the time and he couldn't keep up. We were debriefing at the end of day two or three, and I asked him, "How are you doing?"

Su Chang said, "Man, I am really suffering."

Kevin said, "Let me check your pack." He picked up Su Chang's day pack and the thing weighed a ton. We're supposed to carry like ten to fifteen pounds, but Chang easily had thirty or forty pounds on his back, plus the gear that his porter was carrying.

I asked him, "Why is your pack so heavy?"

He said, "Well, I have all these things. I just want to make sure I'm prepared for anything."

Then I asked, "So, where else in your life are you carrying around too much shit that's weighing you down and causing you to be tired and making you ineffective when you're off this mountain?"

He paused, then said, "You're right. That's exactly my life. I can't get rid of anything. I keep people around. I keep things around that I don't need. We have old files, old processes, old procedures, old this, and old that. I keep holding on to everything thinking we need to use them and keep them. And they weigh me down and they hold my business back. And you're right. I am always tired. I'm always fatigued at the end of the day."

We continued to debrief on that concept. Everybody got their own lessons out of his lesson. That's the power of debriefing. That's the power of facilitating.

Fast forward to after the Kilimanjaro trip. Chang went home and he cleaned up his business. He cleaned up his office and accelerated his income. He hasn't looked back since. Those seven days on the mountain were very, very powerful for him.

In a sales environment, or any situation where production is critical to the success of the business, holding weekly debriefs is a must. The team should know, not only that they are accountable for their performance but they will be celebrated when they hit or exceed their targets. If you only debrief once a month, you've missed four opportunities to improve your numbers; four opportunities to make corrections in approach or process; four opportunities to motivate and educate your team.

This strategy of regular debriefs is a key component of a true Summit Leader. Done correctly, debriefing both the mistakes made and the challenges won will strengthen your team. If your group, team, or business is continually pulling the lessons of the team, you will ultimately deliver on your values and mission.

The keys to the effective use of debriefing are in setting a safe environment and asking the right questions.

In 2012, Google launched the Aristotle Project, which researched what components or behaviors made up an effective team. They found five primary behaviors—the first being psychological safety. It is defined as how much risk team members perceive and what consequences they believe they may face when asking a question, suggesting a new idea, or owning up to a problem. In essence, it's a person's ability to trust the others on the team.

Setting a psychologically safe environment for a debrief means teaching everyone to look at a situation, good or bad, as a learning experience. Solving the issue is always more important than assigning blame. It means setting clear expectations, i.e., no finger-pointing, no talking trash behind others' backs, no excuses, and no unfounded opinions. The discussion needs to remain on the situation at hand, not the personalities of the people involved. No one person should be allowed to monopolize the conversation. When someone takes ownership and accountability for an issue, they need to be celebrated for standing up; not chastised for the error. As a Summit Leader, it is your responsibility to model these behaviors for your team

Team members are taught how to communicate directly with others outside the debrief when problems arise. I call this 'calling out' and I'll go into it in more detail in the chapter on execution. What is important is to be taught to call out with respect and the goal of making the team and the organization better. Roleplay, practice it, set up worst-case scenarios, which is what we do with sales teams in particular. You stand a person up and have them ask, "Okay, so any questions?" Then you respond, "Yeah, you have no idea what you're talking about. You're an asshole." Now the person has to figure out how to handle it. You role-play the scenario until the person can stay calm and understands how not to get upset when somebody comes after them. We found when we did those kinds of role plays with our sales teams, their numbers would jump through the roof. They'd make twice the number of calls and close twice the number of deals. Why? Nothing else changed. Everything was the same. It's just their mindset was different. They were calm. They weren't reacting, because they had practiced and prepared.

The second key to using debriefs effectively is to ask the right questions. As a leader, a debrief isn't about correcting, advising, lecturing, or even consoling. It's about asking good questions. It's about getting people to understand what happened, why it happened, and to take responsibility for learning something as a result of the experience. The purpose of asking the right questions is to be looking for patterns. Use these seven questions for debriefing any situation.

1. **What happened?** Stick to the facts, not opinions.
2. **Why did it happen?** Facts only – no assumptions.
3. **What worked?** And why did it work?
4. **What didn't work?** Not what went wrong. There is no right or wrong, only what worked or didn't work.
5. **What did you learn?** This is the most important question. You should be looking for patterns of behavior or results, not isolated incidents.
6. **Stabilize the lesson** with the whole team so that the lesson for one becomes the lesson for all.
7. **What can you do to correct it (if it was a mistake) or leverage it (if it was a win)?** This question must be asked last, once you have all the information. Otherwise, you may put something into action that could create more problems than you had to begin with.

Educate and Facilitate

Preparing and training your team requires a Summit Leader to be both a great educator and a great facilitator. I feel it's important to understand what these words really mean.

Education comes from the Latin word 'educere,' which means 'to draw out of.' To draw out of—not to cram into. The idea of education follows the Socratic method of asking questions and soliciting feedback from other people. That's what we do in the debrief tent. We're continually asking questions such as, "What happened? How does that play out in your life? Where does this show up?" Participants come up with great answers and the others in attendance learn from them.

The second part of being a great educator is being a great facilitator. Facilitator comes from the Latin word *facilitare,* which means "to make easy." So, to be a great facilitator is to make learning easy for your team. Don't make it archaic. Don't make it difficult. Schools spend a lot of time making things complicated and it keeps people confused. The strategy is that the ones who can figure it out are smart and they go on to better grades and higher degrees. But everyone needs to learn, not just the ones who can memorize a lot of information and take tests well. And everyone needs to learn how to learn. So, as a facilitator, your job is to make things easier...not harder.

If you continue to look up further definitions of facilitation, you'll find it also means making things easy by lowering resistance. What is resistance? It's the natural response we all have to making changes. It's your Little Voice that says, "It's too dangerous. It's too difficult. I'm too old. I don't want to look stupid. I'm not smart enough." Or perhaps it says, "I'm comfortable where I am right now. I don't want to do anything else." That's resistance. Part of being a great facilitator is asking the questions that will allow a person to spot their own resistance and figure out their own ways of removing it.

Personal Development

The second part of training is personal development to overcome the resistance to making changes. This is critical because most things we want to learn are not that complicated. What makes it difficult to learn is our discomfort with the change.

What causes the resistance to making sales calls? What causes the resistance to openly communicate with other team members? What causes the resistance to lose weight? What do you do when the little voice in your head will not let go? When doubt rises and confidence wanes, how do you break the cycle? These are questions that require personal development education.

Many years ago, Robert and I committed to working obsessively toward our personal and emotional development. And by obsessive, I mean I studied and practiced several times a week, multiple times a month, engaged coaches, read lots of books, watched lots of seminars and videos, and listened to lots of audio programs. We engaged with whatever could get our hands on. What I realized many years ago, was that the cause of most of my problems was me. When I finally understood it at a cellular level, that the one thing in common with everything in my life was me, I became obsessed with figuring out what was going on in my head.

Those years of training have paid off in huge ways. When others thought personal growth programs were on the fringe, we immersed ourselves heavily so that when chaotic economic and social times would come, we would be mentally and emotionally fit for the task.

I know for Robert, it's clearly the best move he's ever made. And we still engage in personal development training whenever we can. We continue to work on ourselves and our issues and things that will make us better. We are confident that personal development is the final frontier.

Technically, the human brain can only go so far and then artificial intelligence takes over. We're already seeing that in the innovations occurring. But when it comes to communication, reason, collaboration, ethics, being able to maintain civility, a standard of living, and quality of life, artificial intelligence can't handle that, at least not now. To be able to get past your own insecurities, to be able to have confidence in talking to other people, to be able to collaborate and solve problems, are the things that humankind needs to learn how to do. Otherwise, we will cease to exist.

Silencing the Little Voice

I spoke earlier in this book about your "Little Voice"—the one that's always telling you not to do things, the one that makes you afraid to take risks, and that tells you you're not good enough. Being able to silence the Little Voice so you can be the person you are truly meant to be is one of the primary reasons for working on yourself.

The Little Voice is an internal vocalization of beliefs, values, or thoughts buried in your subconscious from things you've heard, experienced, read, or were preached that start speaking out loud. It's just your conditioned mechanism for protecting yourself from venturing out of a comfort zone.

That Little Voice has become really good at painting you into the corner you are already in.

On Kilimanjaro, the fear of the unknown is what the Little Voice feeds on. I have a client from a large haircare manufacturer, who expressed this really well. He said, "Time is fertilizer in the garden of the Little Voice." In other words, the more time you have to think about something that causes you fear or worry, the more your Little Voice is going to eat away at you. On Kili, not knowing about the effects of altitude on your body is one of the biggest Little Voice concerns. "Am I going to be warm enough? Do I have the right clothing? Am I going to be able to deal with the altitude and oxygen levels? What happens if my sleeping bag gets wet?" All of these unknowns are fuel feeding the Little Voice.

And more importantly, it saps your energy. It becomes a self-fulfilling problem if you let the Little Voice run rampant or are unconscious to its existence. Learning how to meditate, learning how to be calm, learning how to control your mind, and learning how to be very, very present is critical. It's something you automatically learn when you go up Kilimanjaro, otherwise, you could just have a continual panic attack along the way.

One of my clients in the beauty business, a legend in the hairdressing industry worldwide, who's become a great friend over many years, is a fellow by the name of Chris. He's a great trainer and instructor. He's also a great artist. Thousands of people come from all over the world to watch him cut hair and demonstrate new techniques. He's learned from me to become a master facilitator, a master trainer, one of the best I've ever seen.

But early in our relationship, he wanted to make more money in his business by selling some of his new training products and services. He just couldn't seem to get past a barrier. He set a goal for himself that he wanted to do something simple like $80,000 in sales over a 12-week period in his new product. So, Jason, one of my amazing trainers, ran him through a program we call the Little Voice Mentoring Program.

Jason asked Chris questions about his Little Voice, his opinion about sales, and his opinion about adding value to people. Somewhere about two to three weeks into the seven-week program, Chris realized he never saw himself as a salesperson. He saw himself as an artist because he thought "sales" was some kind of a dirty word. When he really understood that sales was simply helping other people to get what they want, he was able to see it was his Little Voice, his fear of rejection, that was holding him back.

Long story short—within six weeks Chris did $200,000 in sales, once he got past his Little Voice that said, "I don't sell." He had never realized that the self-sabotaging Little Voice was what was holding him back. He just felt he wasn't good in sales. Getting your Little Voice out of the way can have dramatic results.

Just to be clear, let me give you an example of the difference between a debilitating Little Voice and an empowered voice. Read these two statements and ask yourself how they make you feel. These are part of the foundational brilliance of the book *Rich Dad Poor Dad* and the Rich Dad principles:

"I can't afford it."

"How can I afford it?"

The first is a statement that comes from a sense of lack (Little Voice). The second is a question that comes from a sense of power.

Say to yourself, "I can't afford it." There's a hard stop in your brain, a futile giving up kind of thinking. I'll even bet your energy level drops, and some negative emotion pops up.

Now, say to yourself, "How can I afford it?" Your brain automatically kicks into gear looking for answers, working on all sorts of ways to come up with a solution. Your energy, inquisitiveness, and creativity all go to work coupled with a sense of hope.

By overriding and reprograming our Little Voices to ask the right questions instead of following old, conditioned responses, we get the right answers. Example: Question: "How can I afford it?" Answer: Learn how to SELL. Sales equals Income. If I want a better lifestyle, I simply have to create more income (active or passive) to make it happen.

By asking yourself the right questions, you will get the right answers. By making the proper declarations to yourself, you will end up with the results you want. But it's not as easy as it sounds. Like everything else worth doing, it takes practice. Lots of practice. Our Little Voices have been with us a long time. They aren't anxious to leave. Having a mentor or coach who can help you discern between what's possible and what your Little Voice is telling you, goes a long way toward silencing them.

Nothing's Perfect

One of the Little Voices that shows up for a lot of people is the one that tells you something has to be perfect before it can be done. Perfection is your Little Voice's way of making sure you don't move out of your comfort zone, you don't take risks, you don't move forward. As long as you keep working at something, you're making progress, right? Or is it a protective mechanism to keep you "working on it" and out of the firing line? Remember, no one can say you aren't *trying*....or can they?

I'm here to tell you nothing is perfect. And the need for perfection can lead to holding onto garbage and stagnation. The morning of the first day of the climb we had to weigh our mountain bags. The porters are not permitted to carry more than forty pounds for safety and health reasons. Many of us were carrying too much gear and we had to offload items that were making the bags heavy. However, some, like Su Chang who we talked about earlier, felt compelled to hold on to his stuff. On the mountain, ounces equal pounds, and pounds equal pain!

The lesson for everyone was clear. Holding on to your stuff or holding onto perfection, whether physical, emotional, or mental, will ultimately take its toll. You must be willing to shed things in life to get stronger and achieve your goals. The need to have everything perfect around you, all your conveniences, luxuries, and comfort items, can cause you to suffer as you move to higher altitudes in your thinking, operating, and your life.

Let go of perfection. Let go of stuff, shed what you don't need down at the base, and create energy and space for what will show up at altitude.

Team members create "stuff" around them to keep them comfortable where they are. If you want to summit your team, you have to encourage them to let go of some of their stuff. Old ideas, worries, assumptions, unnecessary gear and even friends who drag you down.

You, as a Person, Matter

In 2019, I had an amazing opportunity when I was in Thailand to go to one of the largest Buddhist temples in the world. I had the greater fortune of being able to sit and talk with the senior abbot monk who literally presides over hundreds of thousands of people meditating every week. It was very enlightening.

He wrote a book that he gave to me called *Train the Trainer*. In his book, he talks about three things I feel it is important for all leaders to understand, particularly those who want to be great teachers.

The first is to understand **what** it is you are teaching. Is it relevant? Is the material you are teaching or instructing people important for their success? Does it match their needs? Is it a fit? Have you broken it down properly? We talked about that earlier—creating processes.

He went on to say that what you are teaching is not as important as the second thing. Number two is **how** you teach; the way you teach. In the Blair Singer Training Academy, we've developed a process of training over the last twenty years that is second to none. We take average people and turn them into some of the most extraordinary facilitators and educators, some of the best trainers, in the world. The monk said the **way** you teach is more important than **what** you teach. I'll say it again. The way you teach is more important than what you teach.

But there is something even more important than the way you teach. The third and most important element is **who** you are as a person. When you take a position of leadership, people naturally are watching every move you make; not because they like you or don't like you, not because they are looking for faults; it's just how human behavior works. Understand that right now as you're reading this, if you're a leader, you are the subject of dinner conversations at other people's dinner tables, whether you like it or not.

So, the most important thing he told me is who you show up as. What kind of person you are is the most important; your authenticity, your integrity. Do you really walk the talk of what you're talking about? Because people take their cues from you as a leader.

I received a lifetime of learning from this monk during the few hours I spent with him. I've never forgotten it. It's what I teach all my trainers; what I teach every leader. The most important piece is not the content, it's not the technical part, it's the context or the way you teach it, the environment you teach in, and even more importantly, it's who you are as a person. Who you are will speak louder than any words you will ever say.

A leader who assumes the role of also being a great teacher and facilitator becomes a great mentor and an inspiration to everyone on the team. The lessons of authenticity, integrity, and responsibility are priceless. As a teacher/leader, who you are as a person, the example you set for your team, turns out to be the greatest teacher of all.

Chapter Eleven

Execution

"Vision without execution is hallucination."
—Thomas Edison

"Rest step...pressure breathe...Rest step...pressure breathe." At the constant reminder of our guides, this is our mantra. It is the unweighting of one leg while resting your body on the skeletal structure of your stepping leg. It is the lip pursing forceful exhaling that expels the unwanted CO_2 from your system to allow the precious oxygen molecules a place to land in your bloodstream.

Kilimanjaro is summited one step at a time. One of the rules is to never ask the guide what tomorrow's hike is going to look like. Never ask about the weather, what the summit is like, etc. It's wasted information and can cause you to throw your Little Voice into loops of wonder, anxiety, and energy-zapping stress.

Execution is following operating procedures with excellence and care. It is putting focused action into the plan to achieve your mission and values. Anyone can bark out orders to be followed. To be a Summit Leader, to achieve the highest levels of performance, requires a leadership style that includes more people skill than technical. The following actions will make you more comfortable.

Mistakes Push You Forward

Success is simply a series of mistakes that are acknowledged, learned from, and corrected along the way. Any time you move from the known into the unknown or into a project where experience is low, this is the case. That is why rules must be tight. They reduce the amount of variance possible. The rule is this: the tighter the tolerance, the higher the performance. Here is an example:

My first car was a 1963 Chevy and the maximum speed was about 60 miles per hour. You could fix it with a crescent wrench and a screwdriver if it broke down. On the other side of the equation, my wife worked for Northrop Grumman. They made F-18 fighter planes. The rivets were packed in dry ice before they were inserted into the fuselage. Why? Because in order for that plane to fly at two to three times the speed of sound, the manufacturing tolerances must be very tight. If you tried to move a '63 Chevy through space at Mach 3, it would disintegrate. An F-18 traveling at 50 mph down the runway will never get off the ground. The F-18 requires tighter tolerances for increased performances.

When life and death are on the line, like on Kilimanjaro, you cannot afford to make too many mistakes. In other words, when I got stopped at Stella Point because I made the mistake of taking medicine when I shouldn't have, there was no tolerance for that mistake. I had to be sent down immediately. I couldn't wait it out, figure it out, see if it works, because my life was on the line.

When the Apollo 13 crew went to the moon and one of the oxygen tanks exploded, the crew had to figure out how to fix it. They had a low tolerance for making a mistake at that point because there were three lives at stake—theirs. Any one mistake could have caused a catastrophic failure, but knowing what was at stake, they succeeded.

Therefore, it is critical, as a leader, to build a tolerance for making mistakes. Everyone makes mistakes eventually, and you as a leader need to be able to acknowledge and move on from those mistakes. But you also have to know, however, that as your performance goes up, the tolerances for some of those early mistakes becomes less and less. Not just your mistakes, but also the mistakes of your team. Sales and marketing are a continual trial-and-error process. If you are looking for immediate streamlined results in those areas, you will be disappointed. However, if your team debriefs effectively and then tests and retests, you will take on an enthusiasm and energy of being willing to break it again and again as part of your process for achieving higher performance.

Energy is not just high-fiving and telling each other they are awesome. That's okay, but energy comes from reminding others why they are doing what they are doing. Stirring their deep-seated values. It comes from a connection with others.

This can be rough because we are not taught this way in school. We are taught to dread and feel stupid when we make mistakes. We are taught that smart people get it right and dumb people get it wrong. Yet, every entrepreneur KNOWS that in their mistakes are the seeds to their next success.

I'm not saying mistakes are all okay, because sometimes they're not. It depends on what's on the line. What you can tolerate. But if you've been practicing up until then, if you're okay with making mistakes, if you're okay with correcting, if you don't take it personally, if you don't let your ego get in the way, these are the things you, as a leader, can help your team learn. Then, when crucial mistakes occur, you'll correct much more fluidly.

Look, you're never going to stop making mistakes. Early in your life, as a teenager, you made a lot of mistakes. You hung out with the wrong crowd. You did stupid things. But as you got older, your mistakes start reducing in amplitude and in size. Dr. Buckminster Fuller talked about this in terms of the guidance systems on ships and aircraft. These guidance systems use gyroscopes and electronics. The ship at sea is constantly deviating from starboard to port, starboard to port, back and forth, because of the wind and the waves that are moving it off course. The same is true of aircraft flying at high speeds over the earth. They are constantly making mistakes and correcting. My point is, they're making more mistakes, but with a lower amplitude.

Mistakes never go away. Dr. Fuller pointed out that there's no such thing as a straight line in the universe, which is one of the reasons he had such a big impact on me. Mistakes are how you learn. You're never going to get rid of them. Perfection does not exist. What you do is continually fine-tune. You minimize them. I believe it was said that Apollo's space shot was only on course 5% of the time. The rest of the time it was correcting, correcting, correcting.

If you are going to be a Summit Leader, it is important to understand that mistakes are how we learn. We have been taught to be traumatized by them; to be embarrassed by them. Our egos are hypersensitive to them. Hence the need for personal development training that teaches you how to eliminate the trauma and stress.

Of course, you can only learn from mistakes if you take the time to acknowledge them, analyze them, and hold people accountable. Reconvening the team in a high frequency manner and debriefing the wins and mistakes, will accelerate learning and performance.

Accountability Starts with You

There is a crisis of accountability in this country today. It's become too commonplace, too normalized, to place blame, pass the buck, and make excuses. If you truly want a high-performance team, you need to hold them and yourself accountable. This is another area where leading by example pays dividends.

Often people use the words responsibility and accountability interchangeably. But they aren't the same. Responsibility is something you have to do as part of your job, your role, or your commitments. Accountability is how we **behave** when something goes wrong with the things we're responsible for.

As a leader, how do you behave when you've made a mistake or a poor decision? Do you own it in front of your team? Do you ask the same questions of yourself about what worked, what didn't, what can I learn, how can I correct it for the future? I spoke in the last chapter about the need for psychological safety. This is critically important if you want people to feel free to take accountability for their actions. When you model the behavior, you are giving them that psychological safety.

In the years I was in the air freight trucking business, I made a lot of mistakes for a lot of reasons. I'm not justifying them, just admitting to making a lot of mistakes. I made decisions that worked and some that didn't. But the one thing I learned was to own my mistakes and stand up in front of my warehouse crew and my drivers and say, "Look, this initiative that we set out to do is just not working."

I'll give you an example. We moved tractor trailers across the United States and loaded them with all types of cargo from many different customers. Obviously, the more cargo we could get in the trailer of a truck, the more money we could make because we only paid by the mile for that truck to go from, let's say, Los Angeles to Chicago or New York. So, the more we could cram into the truck, the more profit we'd make. I had this great idea that I would share the profitability of each trailer with the whole loading crew. It worked! We upped the amount of weight on each trailer and they became amazingly profitable.

The problem was when those trailers would get to the destination and you opened the door, you could barely get the freight out. It was crammed in there so tightly. And when you did get it out, some of it was broken and damaged. We had to pay OS&D claims (overage, shortage, and damage) to the customers. It cost us a lot—way more money than we made. That was a mistake; a well-intentioned idea, but a mistake.

So, I met with the team and told them, "I screwed up. You guys did a great job. I made a mistake." Then I told them what happened and owned the mistake as mine. Were they upset that I had to take the incentive away? No. They laughed. They thought it was funny. We were in it together.

Sometimes a warehouse person would put the wrong label on a box and sent it to Miami instead of Memphis. Big oops! But they would come to my office and own it, "Boss, I just made a mistake. I didn't know the airport code. I put the wrong label on the box."

"Thanks for letting me know...We'll get it rerouted." We were able to recover from those mistakes. No shouting matches. No calling anyone an idiot or shaming them. I set the example of owning my mistake and calling myself on it as quickly as I could.

Accountability is uncomfortable. It threatens our natural tendency toward self-preservation. But when you get your team on board with being accountable, it will promote growth, improve performance, and each member of the team will gain respect. Embracing accountability can give you more confidence and less fear.

In business, and particularly in sales, accountability is everything. Weekly debrief meetings aren't simply about mistakes and learning from them, but an assessment of how closely your goals have been met for the week. As you know, my experience is mostly in sales. So in my weekly debriefs with the team, I'm asking questions like how many calls did you make; how many people did you see; how many sales did you have, and what revenue was generated?

We measure it on a weekly basis because it gives us the ability to make corrections quickly. Accountability is a very, very big part of execution because if you can't measure it, it's hard to improve it. That's true not just in sales but in all areas of your business.

I liken holding weekly debrief meetings to calling a timeout in the NBA. Think about it. How long does it take to play the last two minutes in a pro basketball game? It can take more than ten minutes because the coaches are constantly calling a timeout. The reason is they want to make corrections to how the team is playing as it's happening.

The same approach should be taken in business. You don't want to wait until the momentum is moving you in the wrong direction and then call a timeout because now the momentum is working against you. One of the things about momentum is that it takes a while to build it, but you can lose it pretty quickly. When you lose it, it takes a long time to build it back up. That's why closely monitoring accountability and continual training are so important.

One of the pitfalls of the debrief that you must look out for are people who don't want to be held accountable. They will hide. In other words, if they don't have the sales numbers or their numbers aren't consistent, they seem to have a "good reason" why. Be cautious of "good reasons" particularly if they keep showing up. Sometimes a team member may say, "I didn't get the numbers, but here's what I learned. I really learned a lot which is a win." Be careful again. Learning a lesson is great as long as it affords correction.

So, as a leader, it's a teaching moment, and also a moment of accountability. As a teacher and a leader, it's important to point out... "It's great that you learned from his week. But the reality is that learning doesn't put revenue on the table unless you make the correction. Let's see how you do next week!" If all they do is learn, they'll soon be learning how to compose a resume and fill out a job application someplace else.

Call It

Accountability isn't just to oneself. Accountability extends to the team. Each member is accountable for the team's overall success. Which means each member has the responsibility to hold every other member accountable. In highly effective teams, the job of holding others accountable does not solely sit on the shoulders of the leader.

When someone breaches the Code of Honor, it is the duty of the team member who saw the breach to "call it." The team has to police itself. It sounds easy, and it can get to be easy once team members respect and trust each other. But in the beginning, it will be hard. Learning how to call a breach requires the leader teaching the team the courage and the skill needed to confront each other with the truth. I go into great detail on how to make a call and how to be the recipient in my book, *Team Code of Honor* if you'd like some help in training your team.

On the mountain, Kristen has no problem calling anybody out on anything if they step out of line. It's something you can count on. She does it with a very high level of intensity, but also with a high level of care. So, while you may be getting scolded, you don't feel like you're being yelled at. You feel like you're being nurtured at the same time. She's very masterful at doing it.

Kevin, on the other hand, is great at acknowledgment. You'll be working and sweating and trudging along and not feeling good. He'll sidle up and say, "Great job. Way to work! You're doing great. Keep going. Only ten more minutes to the next break." He's really good at observing people. I call it calibrating—being able to calibrate how another person is doing and know the right thing to say at the right time that will keep them going, or the right thing at the right time that will call them out or correct them without destroying them. That's an art form. Learning the skills of how to acknowledge and how to call it are priceless. On the mountain, it is the difference between getting the whole team to the top or only just a few strong individuals.

Why is it so important to call it? First, it heads off negative behavior that impedes performance. It also builds character, honor, and pride by engendering a spirit of being willing to do what we agree to do. It becomes something that binds the team together. But the bigger reason is what happens when there are rules in place, someone breaks them, and no one says anything. The team sees that the rules don't matter, they start to implode and revert to a cynical every-man-for-himself attitude. Often, you'll get covert actions to get even with the rule breaker. Sloppy behavior turns into poor results and nasty energy. If you have a code, you have to be willing to risk momentary discomfort by calling it to reap the rewards of a championship team later.

As I said in the accountability section, as a leader you must model the behavior you want to see. If you breach the code or if your behavior goes out of line, (as it will since we are all human) you must be willing to call yourself on it to the rest of the team. Calling others is one thing, but the most powerful thing a leader can do is call it on themself. If you do it publicly, in front of your staff, and say, "Yes, this is something we agreed to and I blew it. I apologize, and here's how I'm going to correct it," people will take you seriously. They will see you as a role model. Even more important, they will learn from you how to call themselves.

Acknowledgment

Calling it shouldn't be used only for negative situations. You can also call it when someone does something exemplary, extraordinary, or just darn nice for another team member. It's as important to acknowledge and celebrate the wins as it is to correct the breaches.

Use lots of real, honest-to-goodness, non-smoke-in-your-face acknowledgment. Our guides were continually saying, "Good job, you guys! Way to work! You got this." Acknowledgment of our struggle pumped energy and life into tired legs, lungs, and Little Voice-infested brains. Delivered consistently at the right times, acknowledgment is powerful.

How often do you acknowledge your team? Only at the successful completion of a task? Or along the way as they struggle and push in search of success? Acknowledging them for everything dilutes true acknowledgment. Too much is too much and becomes counterproductive.

But giving encouragement and recognizing effort along the way, rather than only at the end, increases the motivation and productivity of the team. You acknowledge for something you perceive is a win, particularly if the team or the team member doesn't see it. Your praise for a win they didn't recognize will give them a new perspective, a new view of their job or role. Teaching your team how to celebrate even the smallest of wins reinforces winning activity.

Connection

A very powerful phenomenon occurs with all Mountain Leadership Experience teams. When a person is not feeling so well, perhaps tired, nauseous, light-headed, or struggling, Kevin, one of our lead guides, will pull up next to them while we are walking and just start talking to them. Talking about their life, where they are from, etc. Guess what? The pain and struggle mysteriously go away. I thought it was strange at first. But over the course of nine years of doing this, I have experienced and observed it again and again.

You see, we are creatures who crave connection. In fact, it is a neuroscientific phenomenon. In *Social: Why Our Brains are Wired to Connect*, author Matthew Lieberman says that peoples' "need to connect is as fundamental as our need for food and water."

There is an energetic healing process that occurs when climbers connect and share. The further into isolation you go, the worse you feel. Think about that. With quarantines and isolations, like the current COVID pandemic, the levels of depression, despair, and even suicide skyrocket. Why? Because we have lost the most healing element of all...connection with other human beings who crave the same thing.

Humanity is being challenged to a new standard in this fast-paced world of rapidly changing technology. More and more we become over-automated and digitally driven. How we make and develop connections with our team and our clients will play a large role in our success.

Team members do not want to be treated like just another cog in the production wheel of your organization. They want to be heard and they want to be seen. The same is true of your customers. It's important to be focused on the numbers and the mission. But it's equally important to focus on human connection. As Maya Angelou said, "People won't remember what you said or did; they will remember how you made them feel."

How much attention are you paying to your team or your clients? How many true conversations are you having that aren't business related? How well do you know them? How much time are you spending building relationships?

I think one of the key elements to being a great connector is being an excellent listener. If you go back to the example of the investment bankers who couldn't understand why the phone call with their client didn't go well, you'll see how true this is. They were so focused on getting another sale, they failed to listen to what the client was telling them. They were being asked to help solve the client's problem, but all they heard was an opportunity to line their own pockets. The call failed because they failed to make a connection.

As you grow your business, as you strive to put together a championship team, don't forget your greatest asset is your people. Offer to help wherever you can and don't be afraid to ask for help.

Make meaningful connections and lead with value.

Know When to Change

Any bullheaded entrepreneur can keep going. The stubbornness that makes you successful, however, can also create lots of collateral damage. Sometimes, the hardest thing to do is to STOP. On Kili, stubbornness can be fatal. In business, it can ruin your health and your family if you let your drive become too much of an obsession.

Years ago, on one of our first Mountain Leadership Teams, a very successful entrepreneur and dear friend from Singapore got to Stella Point just as I had but was very weak. Because his blood oxygen was also low, he was told he could not go to the summit. He got angry and upset. He started to argue with Kristen. "I can make it. I can do it. I can push my way through this!"

Kristen replied, "You will not go. Your oxygen is too low. You may make it there, but you may not make it back. So, you're not going."

I went up to him and said, "Look, Richard, this mountain's not going anywhere. It'll be here next year and the year after, and long after you and I are both gone. I love you. And I want you to be safe. I want you to be the best." I gave him a kiss on the head. He went down the mountain. Little did I know that a few years later, I'd be sitting in the exact same place. You've got to know when to stop.

I learned the lesson of stopping from watching Richard, Kevin and Kristen, and others. Phil Knight, one of the co-founders of Nike said it really well. "Sometimes quitting is genius." Unfortunately, we're taught never to quit. Well, sometimes, quitting is the best thing to do; to regroup and fight another day. Otherwise, you could take your whole team down with you, your family, all your resources, and even your life. So, knowing when to change is one thing, but knowing when to quit is a dramatic extension of that.

So, how do you know when too much is too much? You simply need to TRUST yourself. Your body, mind, and spirit are programmed to let you know when things need to change. Listen to them.

A big lesson for me as the leader and facilitator of the climbing group was trust. In prior trips and other situations, I tended to stress a bit about how to best lead the team, what things I should plan for them, etc. This time, I let things develop on their own and simply observed, facilitated, and drew the lessons from the team itself. It was magical to simply observe, sense, feel, trust, and respond.

In speaking with one of my personal coaches, he made an observation that struck home. The more wins you get in your life and the more success you have in areas that are important to you, the more of yourself you have. In other words, your awareness, your power, your abilities, and your perceptions become keener. As a result, you are better able to trust life one moment at a time.

There is no stress in present time…only in the perception of the future or in memory of the past. So, I learned that celebrating all wins not only builds energy, it restores lost life force. On Kili, there is enough life force to power a civilization, but you have to be present to take it in. Each moment is a win. Each moment is a reclaiming of your powers, your sensitivities, your perceptions, and your connectedness. The more of YOU there is, the more you trust yourself.

Pressure can be Positive

In business, when pressure is added to a system, it creates stress. It creates emotion. People don't like it, and they run away from it. They become risk-averse, when the truth of it is, in the right environment a leader can apply pressure and the team will evolve to a higher, more capable team. (Provided the leader has taught the team how to deal with stress and how to master the Little Voices in their heads telling them everything is a disaster.)

Under pressure, people normally want to do one of three things. They run in the opposite direction—fight or flight. Number two is they self-medicate somehow. It could be drugs, alcohol, shopping, whatever, they just want to mask it. They don't want to deal with it. The third thing people do is they allow the pressure to dissipate in a way that's not constructive. In other words, they get angry, they scold, they become abusive.

This is why having a Code of Honor is important. It protects them from themselves because under pressure, emotions are going to go up and intelligence is going to go down. Most of us don't make good decisions when we're angry or stressed.

But pressure isn't always bad. In fact, it's necessary for a team to evolve. If you're not driving ahead, if you're not putting some sort of pressure on the team, you're standing still. And if left alone, the team will ultimately be like a tree that falls in a forest. It'll just decay. It'll just dissipate.

There have been many studies of retired executives and individuals who were in highly mission-driven positions. Once they retire, even in full health, if they don't take on another mission, or they don't take on some other tasks, their life expectancy is significantly shortened. It's nature's way of saying, okay, well, you're not in motion anymore, so you're not needed anymore.

Some amount of pressure can be positive for the growth and development of your team. It's up to you as a Summit Leader to ensure they are prepared and trained to handle it.

Have Fun!

You have to have fun. If it's all serious, all the time, no one is going to want to stay a part of the team, no matter how firmly they believe in the mission and values. You need to be able to laugh, particularly under pressure.

On Kili we have fun. We laugh a lot. We cry a lot. And we laugh some more. Your ability to look at the crazy side of things and to step outside and watch yourself is always very powerful. It's one of the reasons why we debrief at the end of the day. You hear, "Oh, I had a rough day today. It was tough," or "I'm feeling like garbage." Yet, the ability to step outside yourself and look at your situation and even observe where this situation shows up in other areas of your life, can be liberating. It sometimes becomes almost a joke. So, the mountain is there to teach you something you did not expect to learn.

On the mountain, everyone gets a nickname. My son was Sleeping Beauty because while most of us had trouble sleeping at higher altitudes, he would crash at 7:30 and sleep like a rock until 6:30 the next morning. It made for lots of laughs. Mine was Pee Bottle because it took me two days to finally use one at night in my tent rather than getting dressed and having to go out and weather the freezing cold.

Laughter breaks the tension. It keeps you human. It reminds you nothing is so big that you can't enjoy laughing about yourself and each other.

Chapter Twelve

The Summit Is Not It!

*"The greatest lesson that nature is now trying to teach humanity
is that when the bumblebee goes after its honey,
it inadvertently pollenates the vegetation...
at 90 degrees to the bumblebee's aimed activity."*

—R. Buckminster Fuller

At 11:38 am Tanzania time on the third of July 2013, my son Ben and I hit the summit sign at Uhuru Peak—19,341 feet. We hugged, we cried, we cheered. It was a loooonnng journey that had started with a school prank gone awry, an aborted climb the year before, and this final ascent.

In my backpack, I had an engraved pendant and key chain for Ben. In that rarified air, I gave it to him. On one side it said:

"Kilimanjaro 2012-2013"

On the other side,

"We start together and we finish together." – Dad

When I gave it to him I told him that I would always have his back.

That climb changed my life. Not getting to the summit, but the journey.

Every climber will tell you it's never about the summit. It's about the amazing physical, emotional, and spiritual transformation that occurs from the moment you decide to go there. It's about feeling the Earth rotate under your feet as you watch the curve of the horizon drop to reveal the sun on a summit morning.

There is always a moment of exhilaration and celebration at the top. But those aren't the feelings that remain. It's the lessons of leadership, health, connection, love, and awareness that stay with each person forever. The summit is not the real goal. It's only the goal that takes you on a journey to find your best self.

For a true Summit Leader and their team, it's not about the goal. It's about all the stuff you learn on the way. It's about the ripple effect of everything you do that radiates out from the experience. The impact you have. The people you meet, the lessons and insights you learn, the connections you make, the strength, the friends, the love, the institution you build, the comradery that's formed in building it.

I became a real father there, on that first climb when I chose to follow my personal Code of Honor and follow my sick son back down the mountain.

The summit is simply a byproduct of taking one step at a time. One breath at a time...over and over and over. Summitting is a momentary win. A milestone event. But the whole experience is so much more than that.

The summit itself is actually anti-climactic. There is a sadness that seeps into the team at the top. The journey that started months ago is now over, and everyone turns their minds and spirits homeward. The unity of the team begins to dissipate. We take our pictures at the summit and descend. In my opinion, having an anti-climactic feeling after successfully attaining a goal is one sign of a really good team. They're ready for the next thing, asking, what do we do now? If you give a team like that a little training, you can accomplish anything.

So how do you keep your teams motivated? How do you keep them striving? I am sure you have experienced the momentary letdown that occurs after the achievement of a goal. What if I told you it is supposed to be that way? We've been taught our entire lives that goals are important. Goals are important because they give you direction, control over your life, and cause you to step up to bigger and bigger challenges. But attaining a goal isn't the end game. It's the ripple effect of your journey toward that goal that is the source of infinite returns...not the goal itself.

Precession

Dr. Buckminster Fuller explained this by describing the role of the bumblebee. The bee emerges from the hive every day to go searching for flowers to gather nectar to make honey, which it needs for its food and survival. In the process, it cross-pollinates other flowers, plants, and vegetation. It seems clear that the bee's greater purpose is to pollinate because it sustains life on planet Earth.

Bumblebee and Flower with True Purpose

Is the bee's goal to make honey the real goal? No! The real goal is to pollinate, but the bee doesn't know that.

We are really no different than the bee. We go out every day to make money. What do we need the money for? We need it for food and shelter, the same thing the bee needs honey for.

But often, once you achieve a goal you've set for yourself, a strange thing happens.

Let's say you want to make $10,000 in sales this month. You make it and everyone celebrates. But it's not quite good enough. You set a bigger goal... $20K next month, and $30K the month after that, and after a while reaching the goal seems to get harder. You plateau, and maybe even experience a diminishing return.

Or, maybe you have a big win. You win an award. You achieve some great recognition. You give a great presentation, and you receive glowing accolades and have great sales. But over the next day or so, you begin to feel a bit of a letdown.

Why is that?

Dr. Fuller says the goal is not the main point. It is the ripple effect, or what he calls the "precession" of going for the goal, that is the main point. The bee pollinates. That is the precession of seeking honey. The true purpose.

The true purpose of summiting Kilimanjaro is that you become a better leader, a better teammate. You become more aware. You can handle more adversity which reflects in all areas of your life: physically, mentally, emotionally, and spiritually. Rewards that last a lifetime.

YOU→ Goal/$ (apparent goal) and Infinite Returns as the Precession

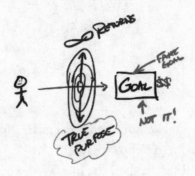

The bigger reason for setting goals is not for the achieving of those goals, which, by the way, is great to do. But the bigger reason is because, somewhere along the way to that goal, the ripple effect of that journey or precession is going to present to you during the next goal or your bigger purpose.

Let me tell you some stories about a series of goals that were never IT, but the precession, getting to my real purpose, was.

Like many of you, I started out with the intent to simply make money. I had left my hometown in Ohio and moved to Hawaii, mostly because of a beautiful woman I followed there. I got a job at a large Fortune 100 company in sales, almost got fired because I was so bad, but I got better. About the time I had achieved success in that organization, I got introduced to a bunch of crazy entrepreneurs in Honolulu and jumped into partnership with a sailing buddy to start my first business. It was a failure. We had a great time, even though we didn't make any money. But it was a start in a new direction. A new game.

The bigger purpose wasn't about making that business work. It was there I met Robert Kiyosaki who got me involved in personal development education and who became one of my best friends and teachers. As I mentioned earlier, I became intrigued with personal development because it caused me to see that most of the problems and challenges I had in my life were because of me.

Now, I had a new goal: Clean myself up!! If I can clean myself up, I will make all the money I want. On the way to doing that, I got asked to teach some of the programs I was taking. That became the next goal. Plus, I had to keep building my businesses to earn the credibility to teach.

The next new goal was to become the best trainer in the world and transform the marketplace and make lots of money.

I got to the point where I actually went around the world twice in opposite directions in less than ten days because the demand for my time became so great. My mission, which was inspired by Dr. Fuller, was to educate as many people as I could with real business and personal development skills. But I was trading time for money and not making a dent out there. At least not the impact I envisioned. The goal wasn't it.

Robert and I met two amazing individuals along the way named Richard and Veronica Tan who were young new promoters at the time. Today, the Tans' organization, Success Resources, is the largest, most revered business and personal development promotion and production company in the world.

They took a chance and put us on international stages. They introduced us to overseas clients, markets, and companies. The precession of this was I ended up meeting amazing people who kept asking me how I do what I do. They asked me to teach them how to teach.

The precession and the real purpose was, through the Tans' support and through the thousands of programs over the years, to meet, recruit, train, and build a global team of amazing teachers, leaders, and facilitators. These individuals are teaching business skills for entrepreneurs in over thirty countries. They are a part of our Training Academy.

We reach and touch the lives of millions of people, yet we spend very little. We amass millions of dollars of technical, marketing, and program development at very little cost. Why? Because we are a team and the contributions of one serve the whole organization.

Global Organization as True Purpose

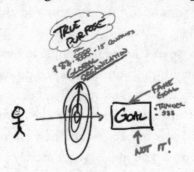

What I am trying to say is that the goal was not it. Being a great trainer was an apparent goal, but the REAL goal turned out to be building a global training organization. This precession, which is usually never in sight in the beginning, has created millions of dollars and countless opportunities for the Training Academy to serve millions of people.

Every member of our team knows the goals they set are never it. They know the flight of the bumblebee. It is the story of the bumblebee that recruited every single one of them into our organization.

Some become great trainers. Some transform entire industries and cultures. Some become the heroes and leaders of their countries. Precession, purpose.

So, what have been the returns from all these temporary goals?

Royalty and license fees from books, programs, videos, subscriptions, etc.

Resources—millions of dollars of technical, program, and business development created by the mission-driven members of our global team.

The building of valuable intellectual property through the wins, failures, and learning experiences of the entire team.

Travel and connection to the most amazing places in the world with the most incredible people whom we call friends and partners.

Connections and joint ventures that reach millions of people without spending millions.

Finding the love of my life at one of the first programs I taught, where I was so bad I literally got booed off the stage.

Best friends, teachers, coaches, and teammates in the world.

The ability to play a game much bigger than myself.

And it all started with a goal of moving to Hawaii.

The good news is returns and opportunities are waiting for you too. Precession is a fundamental law of nature. Every time you drop a stone in the water, it sends out ripples. You have to look for it. It may be at ninety degrees to your focus but it's there. When you find it, you will reap _____ returns. You will be doing what needs to be done.

Maybe you're thinking...Blair, why didn't you just set your original goal to building a global training organization?

Answer: Because I'm not that smart.

Our path as human beings is to learn by trial and error. Through making tons of mistakes, we end up learning the proper direction. Dr. Fuller said we have a right foot and a left foot. Not a right foot and a wrong foot. We make a mistake to the right and to the left and end up moving forward. That is our journey.

The purpose of a goal is ONLY TO KEEP YOU IN MOTION as if it were a magnet drawing you in. The top of Kilimanjaro, your next sales goal, the business you are trying to build, is a magnet to pull you there. Unlike the bee, however, who never knows it is pollinating, you can see the precession of what you are doing. You can get glimpses of the higher purpose or the next task.

If the bee never comes out of its hive, it will die. If you don't do anything, you stay home, or you retire without taking on some other goal, another worthy game of some sort, nature has a funny way of checking you out. Health can deteriorate. You get older faster. Vision dims. Life expectancy shortens. You get checked out.

We are supposed to be in motion. Why? Because we have a greater purpose to accomplish. You have a function in the scheme of life to fulfill, just as the bee does. The only way to find it is not by sticking your finger in your navel and wishing for it (although that may work for some people). It shows up during your quest for goals. Even though the goal is never 'it.' IF the goal were it for the bee, after a few flowers it would quit and die.

If making that $10K was it, you would stop, and there would be no higher purpose and you would check out. You would get bored and depressed until you found another goal to put you in motion. It's all about precession.

Fuller said in order to see the next game or purpose, it's best not to look at the world from the perspective of right or wrong, good or bad.

The first forging of metals was undoubtedly used for making swords and weapons for killing people (not great). However, that same technology was then used to make steel plows to till the soil and feed more people (better). Was forging metal good or bad? Neither and both.

COVID-19—Good or bad? Bad—It kills people. Good—We learned human beings love and crave connection, which we saw at an unbelievable rate through the internet. We also learned there is a ton of bad information out there, which means the need for great teachers and leaders is important. That's good. It will lead to more successful businesses, medical professionals, service providers, and people who really know what they are talking about who will become the next generation of leaders.

There are plenty of teachers who claim to be able to help the average entrepreneur succeed. Many claim to teach the secrets to wealth, success, and happiness. However, at the end of the day, most of them are better salespeople than they are teachers. They don't have the real-life experience of facing difficult challenges. They may claim to make you a YouTube millionaire, but they can't teach you the skills of how to get up when you get knocked down, how to face an economic meltdown, how to deal with staff members who won't cooperate, how to protect your assets, mainly because they haven't experienced those situations. In the thirty-plus years I have traveled the world, I have encountered tons of misinformation, sales hype, and promises that lure hardworking entrepreneurs to spend precious money that produces very little. These are fake teachers.

True teachers are leaders. The **way** they teach is more important than **what** they teach. Who they are as a person physically, mentally, emotionally, ethically, and spiritually has an even greater impact on the student than the content being delivered.

On the flip side, great leaders are also great teachers. They pass the body of their experience to the rest of us so we can BE better. As a leader and teacher, you create a ripple effect/precession wherever you go. It's a huge responsibility, but it creates infinite returns. Dr. Fuller said, "The more people I serve, the more effective I become."

The End of the Game

It was another great teacher by the name of Alan Walter who slid this piece into the equation. In studying the trends of human life, global economics, and human psychology, he observed that when any nation, person, or business falls into depression, it simply signals "end of game." Not end of the world; end of game.

In 1929, after the sky-high Roaring '20s, the U.S. fell into the Great Depression. It stayed in that state for years until a new game materialized called World War II, which led to new prosperity and even higher living standards.

Depression signals end of game.

It was that letdown after the performance, after the achievement. It was not the end of the world. The prior game wasn't it. So, is depression good or bad? Bad because it sucks. Good because it signals time for a bigger and more worthy game.

If you look at your career, you will see that each goal achieved or each obstacle encountered set you on the path to another one. The new goal was always there to present itself but you didn't take it on proactively because you didn't need to.

We don't look at our finances when things are good because we don't need to until we have a crisis. At that point, we are forced to do it. The precession is always out there, the invitations to change are always there, but we don't pay attention.

It's time to take a look at a new game. What's yours?

We have done a good job with the goals we have set over the years of our lifetimes. Some we achieved, some we did not. But what was the precession of all that? Somewhere out there, if you look to your right and left, are the indications of the next new game for you—a new business, a new way to do business, a new set of relationships.

True Purpose of Depression

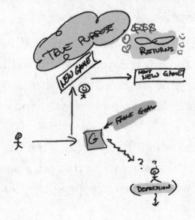

Through this trial-and-error process, if you ever feel down or depressed, remember it's not the end of the world for you. It's not the end of you. It's the end of the game you were playing. It's time for a new game. During COVID-19 we've had to completely flip the model of our business. It's been a great thing, but it was scary and depressing in the beginning.

What are you supposed to be doing?

As long as the bumblebee does what it is supposed to be doing, the bee is just fine. There are plenty of flowers. If you take on the next game, find a new team, take on the next goal, and just go out there and keep yourself in motion, I guarantee the universe will put some flowers in front of you to keep you going.

Chapter Thirteen

Mountain Leadership Experience Lessons

*"The mountain will always teach you a lesson
that you were not expecting."*
—Kevin Cherilla

Remember, the secret to being a Summit Leader is in creating a context or environment that produces extraordinary results and extraordinary teams. I maintain the best leaders are those who have the greatest vision, who can see what's coming down the road, and are able to put their teams in the flow of the progress. The best leaders are those who focus inward as much as they focus outward and work to be the best versions of themselves they can be.

I've given you a ton of food for thought within these pages, so here's a quick summary of what it takes to be a Summit Leader.

1. **Leaders start with their mission, purpose, and a big WHY?**
2. **Leaders use Values** to create expectations, to set rules, and to reinforce beliefs.
3. **Leaders are tireless students** of their own trade and learning outside the box to spark different perspectives.
4. **Leaders are incredibly gracious** to everyone they come in contact with.
5. **Leaders master preparation and the task** and love both parts of it.
6. **Leaders create and identify narrow time boundaries,** shrinking the space so their teams can focus.

7. **Leaders eliminate uncertainty through preparation** and frequent communication.

8. **Leaders see mistakes as learning opportunities,** recognizing that failure is an important piece for true growth.

9. **Leaders create trust and respect** within the team promoting psychological safety.

10. **Leaders have a Code of Honor** to which they and their team adhere. Accountability is a cornerstone of the Code.

11. **Leaders have fun** and give genuine encouragement and acknowledgment to their team.

12. **Leaders value personal development** and know how to master the Little Voices.

13. **Leaders know that the Summit is NOT IT.**

And most important of all.

14. **LEADERS ARE TEACHERS!**

Closing Thoughts

The world, your business, your life and, of course, Kilimanjaro are all filled with challenges. Each one is an adventure, as each involves risk. Yet if there is one thing these experiences have in common that can reduce that risk, it is the relationship you have with your mission, your values, and your team.

As I write this book, the world is facing serious challenges. We all know it. And another thing I know — and I think you do, too — is that all the challenges our world is facing are solvable... by leaders who understand and apply this.

There will always be temptations, delusions, and frustrations that will attempt to lure us away from the right things to do. The things we *know* are right. There are opinions, narratives, false facts, and greed that pepper our journey to the summits of our businesses and our lives. It's not an easy trek.

The world needs better leaders... NOW. Leaders who don't just talk, but leaders who act based on sound principles of truth. Leaders who do not tell others what to do, but leaders who teach others how to think for themselves and who challenge them to become the best version of themselves.

Kilimanjaro teaches a leader how to do those things. She teaches you— in the midst of altitude, changing weather, and sometimes brutal conditions — that, with the right leadership, the journey can be the difference between exhilarating accomplishment or disaster.

The only guarantee on Kilimanjaro is that the person who comes off that mountain will not be the same person who went up. It is an experience that those you lead and influence should share. Their encounters with you should change their lives. Mountain Leadership is the same as Business Leadership.

Keep this book close by and use it as a trail map to take you and your teams to your designated summits. Remember... it's not about the summit itself. What will change all of us is your consciousness of what you do and the results of those actions.

Take on the challenge of leading your teams and show them how to be their best and most amazing selves.

Acknowledgments

Achieving anything great is never a solo endeavor. Climbing Mt. Kilimanjaro is no exception. It requires a team of guides, porters, cooks, tent assistants, and many more. Our team is supported in a way that ensures our success, safety, and well being.

Writing this book is the culmination of the work of all those people on and off the mountain who trained as members of our Mountain Leadership teams. It takes into account the thousands of entrepreneurs in over 40 countries whom I know have put their dreams, their money, and their physical presence on the line to make things happen in their businesses. Sometimes that means putting themselves and their loved ones at great risk.

I am blessed that I have been able to capture a tiny piece of the magic and spirit of Kilimanjaro and parallel her lessons with the life lessons of climbing some of the biggest mountains that each of us face in our lives.

This book is dedicated to the kids in the orphanages where we worked in Tanzania to provide sustenance, education, and facilities for them to grow. Some of their disabilities make the challenges of Kili pale in comparison to the journeys they have to make to survive. It's dedicated to the teams of doctors, nurses, dentists, and interns who travel to Tanzania to volunteer to serve the communities there. To our amazing guides Kristen Sandquist and Kevin Cherilla whose leadership inspired this book and the Mountain Leadership experiences themselves. To our porters, Sistus, Mugumbo, Singa, Nestor, Hassani, Halifa, Veda, Emanuel, Goodlove, Dastan, and Ali under the leadership of Nickson and scores of other porters who make our trek possible. To our Mountain Leadership climbers from over 15 countries, the Blair Singer Training Academy trainers, my great masters and teachers, Dr. Buckminster Fuller, dear friends and colleagues such as Robert Kiyosaki, Kim Kiyosaki, Ken McElroy, Josh and Lisa Lannon, the Warriors Heart team, all the Rich Dad Advisors, my mentors and coaches such as Ceil Stanford, Alan Walter, Monk Bee, Jayne Johnson. Nicole Srednicki and Radha Gopalan who have kept my body younger than my years. Mona Gambetta who has guided me to take my experiences and put them into print. Caren Cantrell who made my ideas readable. Those who molded me early in life and bestowed upon me great values and ethics such as my father and mother, my grandparents, and siblings.

I even acknowledge those who would never dream of an acknowledgement due to the difficult times we encountered together. Each gave me greater strength to learn, correct, grow, and forgive.

Finally... all those great adventurers who set sail on journeys into the unknown or who took on challenges that no one else would face, who stood up to lead in the face of opposition, threats, and even death. For every brave soul who felt there was something that needed to be done and — even when they did not know how to do it — took a step forward in the face of fear.

These are all heroes. They came before us and it is through their journeys and trials that we all stand here today. I am eternally humbled by them and honored to write this book as a tribute to their lessons and examples. May we all make their legacy strong.

About the Author
Blair Singer

The distance between you and the life that you want, is only the distance between your right and left ear. Additionally, the toughest sale of all is you selling you to you. Third, is that any great adventure requires a mission-based, value-driven team. Applying these three principles, Blair has helped change the trajectory of hundreds of thousands of lives and businesses in over forty countries over the last three decades. From pounding the streets as a sales representative in the  early 80's to successful entrepreneur to inspiring the hearts and visions of millions today, his life and career has been an adventure.

Blair is a best-selling author, Rich Dad Advisor and one-of-a kind teacher. His unique messages and unconventional style have supported owners, entrepreneurs and leaders worldwide by helping them increase sales, build champion level teams and make huge differences in their industries. He has worked extensively with organizations like Singapore Airlines, all L'Oreal brands globally, private banks and hundreds of thousands of small and medium sized businesses. His adventure is the journey of the average guy rising above mediocrity to help others find greatness.

In the early 2000's the demand for his teaching was so great that at in less than ten days, he circumnavigated the planet twice in opposite directions! It became clear that the mission of bringing success to the marketplace had to change. Instead, the focus and mission became to 'create the best teachers, leaders and facilitators in the world who could change the way we learn, particularly in the marketplace. He is the founder of the Blair Singer Training Academy and Blair Singer's APEX system which trains and certifies the best change agents in the world. Globally Blair is referred to as the 'Master of Masters' or by those who learn from him... "The Magician."

Having summited Mt Kilimanjaro ten times, he explains that business and life are also adventures that, with the three lessons applied, will take anyone to their summit.

In addition to *Summit Leadership*, Blair is the best-selling author of *SalesDogs®*, *Team Code of Honor*, and *Little Voice Mastery*.

Best-Selling Books in the
Rich Dad Advisors Series

Books by
Blair Singer

Rich Dad Advisor Series Books

Team Code of Honor
The Secrets of Champions in Business and in Life

Summit Leadership
Taking Your Team to the Top

SalesDogs
*You Don't Have to Be an Attack Dog
to Explode Your Income*

Also by Blair Singer

Little Voice Mastery
*How to Win the War Between Your Ears in 30 Seconds or Less —
and Have an Extraordinary Life!*

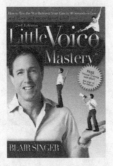

Blair Singer

All the Tools You Need for Entrepreneurial Success

Leads, conversions, raving fans, wealth... and (most importantly) the skills you need to teach others how to replace you.

Here's what's inside...

- **Sales Mastery** – How to put money in your pocket, and teach other people on your team how to do it, too.
- **Team Mastery** – Are you ready to transform regular ordinary people into an income producing championship team?
- **"Little Voice Mastery™"** – How to quiet that "Little Voice" that erodes confidence, creates doubt and keep it from shooting you in the foot.
- **Mastering the Art of Sales and Inner Game of Business**
- **Masterclasses** – Exclusive videos, downloads and training from the people I look to in the areas of health, finance & personal development.
- **Rich Dad Advisors Fundamentals** – Business, finance, money, and more from the most brilliant entrepreneurs I have ever met.
- **And Much, Much More!**

Will these techniques bring you success?

"Using Blair's info I broke $200k in sales for the first time in my biz!!"
-David DuMoulin
Vice President of Engineering at NVIDIA

Visit https://BlairSinger.com/Success for details

Get connected...
and stay connected
with our global
Blair Singer Community

**Visit BlairSinger.com
for**

**News * Blogs
Tools and Resources
Live and Online Events
Podcasts**

Follow Blair on...

[f] *@blairsingerofficial*

[◉] *@blair.singer*

[▶] *@BlairSingerSpeaker*

[in] *@blairsinger*

[🐦] *@blairsinger*

What If You Could Get Out Of The Rat Race And Transition From Self Employed To Fully Scalable Business That Delivers Your Legacy Lifestyle... And Brand That Sells Itself?

Is that an adventure you'd like to go on?

Building your business is like climbing Kilimanjaro, one of the world's top Seven Summits.

Before your expedition starts, you have to plan your ascent, and choose your expedition team. As you ascend, you have to hit certain milestones, and address resistance.
Get it wrong, and reaching the Apex becomes impossible.

Blair Singer's Apex will help you:

- Assess your current business
- Plan your ascent using unique PERT technology
- Assemble your team
- Address resistance
- Master sales, communication, and marketing
- Become a strong business leader and teacher
- Fully scale your business
- Remove yourself from your business, and put even more money in your pocket.

If you are an adventurous entrepreneur ready to scale your business as you would scale Kilimanjaro...